SPORTBIKE SUSPENSION TUNING

Sportbike
Suspension Tuning

HOW TO IMPROVE YOUR MOTORCYCLE'S HANDLING AND PERFORMANCE

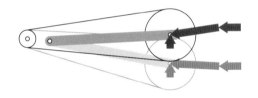

ANDREW TREVITT

DESIGN BY TOM MORGAN

DAVID BULL PUBLISHING

Library of Congress Control Number: 2007928808

ISBN-13: 978 1 893618 45 9
ISBN-10: 1 893618 45 5

David Bull Publishing, logo, and colophon are trademarks of David Bull Publishing, Inc.

Book and cover design: Tom Morgan, Blue Design, Portland, Maine (www.bluedes.com)

Front cover photo credits: Left, Courtesy of Honda; right, Marc Cook; bottom, Courtesy of Ducati.
Rear cover photo credits: Top right, Courtesy of Kawasaki; bottom left; Marc Cook; bottom right, Riles and Nelson.

Printed in Hong Kong

10 9 8 7 6 5 4 3 2 1

David Bull Publishing
4250 East Camelback Road
Suite K150
Phoenix, AZ 85018

602-852-9500
602-852-9503 (fax)

www.bullpublishing.com

RIGHT: Bikes with shaft drive have a different set of forces to deal with, which typically result in too much anti-squat. Manufacturers use various methods to decrease or nullify the effect, such as this BMW layout that employs a parallelogram arrangement. The options for tuning anti-squat in these cases are severely restricted. (COURTESY OF BMW)

PAGE 6: Removing fork oil is one way to address front suspension that is too progressive near the bottom of the stroke. This is discussed in detail in chapter 10. (MARC COOK)

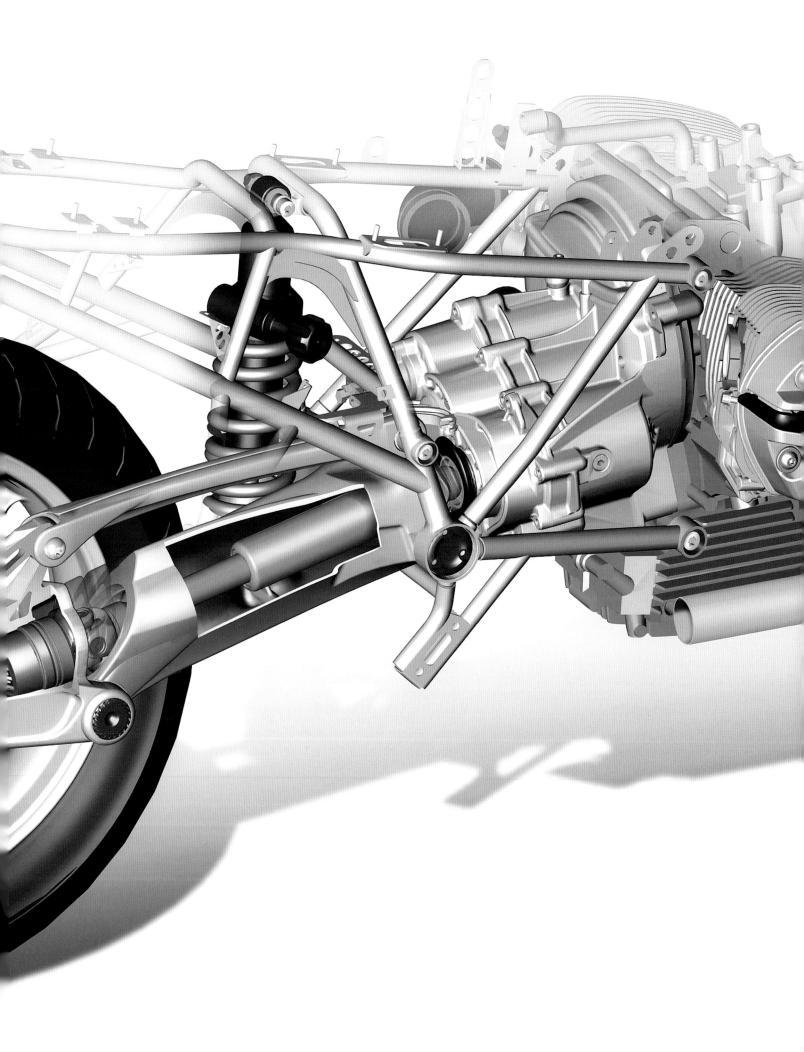

CONTENTS

1. Introduction 9

2. Where to Start 17

3. Basic Principles and Theory 25

4. Geometry and Ride Height 33

5. Springs, Preload, and Sag 43

6. Damping 55

7. Squat and Anti-Squat 79

8. Tires 85

9. Finding a Setup with Stock Components 95

10. Springs, Fork Oil, Fork Oil Height, and Other Mild Modifications 105

11. Aftermarket Upgrades 117

12. Troubleshooting Guide 122

Glossary 126

Index 127

CHAPTER 1

Introduction

f you're reading this, then you've made the first step—the biggest step—toward making your sportbike a better motorcycle, one that is more fun and easier to ride on the street and, perhaps more important for you, quicker around a race track. All this can take place, potentially, without spending a dime on the bike itself. The second step is to overcome your fear of making a mistake adjusting your bike's suspension. Despite the fact that sportbike manufacturers put a lot of effort into developing suspension components that offer adjustments for fine tuning, many sportbike riders will never turn a damping adjuster or preload collar on their bikes, simply because they don't know where to start or are afraid of making their bike handle worse rather than better. This book will guide you through the process of setting up your bike's suspension to suit you and your riding style, from the basics—setting static sag for your weight—to more subtle

OPPOSITE: The author, hard at work racing in the Suzuki SV Cup finals at Road Atlanta in 2003. Suspension tuning is an important aspect of roadracing, and finding a good setup pays off in more ways than just good lap times. (RILES AND NELSON)

and advanced adjustments, such as how to optimize rear-end squat.

The great thing about a sportbike's suspension is that, unlike engine work, you can get started without having to buy any expensive parts. You don't even have to own a full tool chest, as your bike's kit has the basic screwdrivers and wrenches you'll need. You can make some big changes with very little work and even less initial cash outlay—many times I've seen lap times drop by whole seconds after a couple of clicks on a suspension adjuster, an increase in performance that would take thousands of dollars and hundreds of hours of hard work to attain by other means. As your riding improves and you get your bike's setup closer to ideal, you may certainly want to consider expensive aftermarket upgrades, but given the universally high standards of today's sportbike suspension systems, you can go a long way with very little investment when it comes to your suspension.

This book is intended for sportbike riders from entry-level street riders to club racers. Even if you are the most novice of motorcyclists, you can take advantage of a suspension change that makes you more comfortable and confident on your bike. The settings on your bike right now may be suboptimal, or just plain wrong for your weight, riding skill, and style. But if you never make a change or adjustment, how will you know? As your riding progresses, you'll find your suspension needs will change with your skill level. This book will help you adjust your settings accordingly—and, more important, help you understand *why* you're making those changes. We'll talk about the differences between setups for the street and race track and how to optimize your bike for different types of roads and tracks. We'll also discuss how to analyze various handling symptoms and make adjustments to correct them. As you gain riding experience, you may find advantages to replacing or upgrading your stock suspension parts, and this book will help you decide what direction to take with aftermarket components.

My first race bike was a Honda CB175, which my father had modified in true café-racer style with clip-ons, a long tank, a tiny seat, and megaphone exhausts. My only concern with suspension on that particular bike was making sure fork oil didn't leak onto the front drum brake. The CB had no suspension adjustments, and with a whopping 17hp it probably didn't need any. From there I graduated to riding my brother's 1979 Yamaha TZ250, a beast of a bike compared to the little Honda. That bike was a big deal back then because it was one of the first

road racers to have a monoshock rear end. Still, the only suspension adjustment I can remember was a three-position front preload cap, and even then my brother had to stuff quarters underneath the cap to stiffen things up.

As I rose through the ranks from amateur to expert and each new bike I rode had progressively more and more suspension adjustments, I had to learn more about setting up my bike properly for different tracks and changing conditions. Every time I made a jump in my riding, I would have to make a similar step in learning about suspension to keep pace—otherwise there would be little improvement. A simple approach of softer for rough tracks and stiffer for smooth tracks grew to a more studied approach of trial and error and—with a great amount of help from other people—log books and notes of settings and characteristics. Eventually I could tell changes of just a couple of millimeters of ride height, one millimeter of trail, or a half-turn of damping. Copious notes, detailing each change for every practice session or race at a particular track, allowed me to quickly return to the proper settings when I visited a familiar track.

Riding skill and bike setup are two sides of the same coin, and as your ability in one discipline improves you will find advances in the other come

almost naturally. You can ride a wobbling, sliding, head-shaking beast only so fast, no matter how good a rider you are, and the only way to improve your riding—and your lap times—is to make adjustments so that your bike works better. Likewise, if you feel your setup is perfect and doesn't need changing, your riding is the limit to how fast you can go—and because of that good setup, your riding can more easily progress to the next level. Setup and skill will leapfrog each other, in smaller and smaller increments as time goes on, until you are dealing in tenths of a second in lap times and quarter-turn increments in adjustments.

Looking back on my racing career, one mistake I made was not researching the technical aspects of my suspension's inner workings enough. I let other people look after that and instead concentrated on learning how each adjustment made the bike react. But why did some adjustments have such a small effect, given the range of that adjustment? And why did others have drastic consequences for just a tiny change? Had I paid more attention to the technical details—what actually happens inside the fork or shock when you turn the adjuster—I would have been in a better position to go further than the standard adjustments allowed, and better equipped to quickly overcome handling issues. With today's bikes having

even more clickers and knobs, it's especially important to have at least a basic understanding of what each does internally so that you can better decide how to make changes. For that reason, this book explains in some detail what each adjuster physically alters inside the fork or shock and outlines what changes in handling you can expect from that adjustment.

There is more to suspension than just fork tubes and shocks. Your bike's geometry—its rake and trail—plays an integral part, as do tires. All three parts—the suspension, geometry, and tires—work together to make your bike behave in a certain manner and give you a particular feel for the road beneath. It's that feel that gives you confidence that your motorcycle will go fast on the race track or be smoother and

safer on the street. Practically no two riders are alike when it comes to setup, and each rider's desire for a particular feel is based on a number of factors. Some prefer steering quickness to stability, which are quite often mutually exclusive characteristics. Riders with a street-only background will typically want a different setup from those who grew up riding dirt bikes. Some find confidence in stiff suspension and a solid feel; others prefer softer settings for a looser ride. It's not that one setup is right and another wrong, but rather what works best for the rider—what gives him the best feedback and confidence.

Because making a suspension adjustment is simple and takes but a few seconds, it's tempting to make wholesale changes to several things at once. You are almost certain to get lost down that path, as there are an almost infinite number of branches. I like to use an engine-building analogy to keep myself from making too many changes at once or making one drastic change without thinking it through first. When I was racing my Honda CBR900RR, I experimented with cam timing a lot. You probably know, or can imagine, how big a job it is to strip a bike down to the cams, measure timing with a dial gauge and pointer, adjust the sprockets, measure again, and finally bolt everything up. It took me a long time—at least a couple of hours—start to finish. For that reason, I

made darn sure that I researched the change I was going to make and had a good idea of what to expect from it before I even took the fairing off. You don't have to be that paranoid about a single suspension change, but the process should be just as studied and methodical.

The importance of making changes one at a time cannot be stressed enough, and it's just as important that those changes be thoroughly tested and recorded so that you fully understand how a particular change affects the handling of your bike. Too often I've succumbed to the temptation of making more than one adjustment, but the result is always the same: The bike may be better or worse, but which adjustment is responsible? One step forward, two steps back.

Each of the next few chapters deals with a different aspect of suspension, with related troubleshooting help and symptoms to look for when dealing with that particular aspect. Chapter 9 summarizes the process into a step-by-step guide to setting up your motorcycle for a given track, road, or riding style.

CHAPTER 2

Where to Start

inding the ideal setup for your bike can be both a frustrating and rewarding experience. It can take any amount of effort, ranging from one small change to days of testing, before you hit upon the right combination of geometry, tire selection, and suspension adjustments, but when you do it can be pure magic. Suddenly your bike floats over bumps, turns on a dime, and hits apexes with more accuracy than a wire-guided missile. But just as it's possible to sometimes stumble on the perfect setup by accident, it's also easy to turn your bike from that perfect friend into a bucking bronco if you're not careful. This is why it's important to progress in stages, taking your time and documenting everything. Your setup is influenced by geometry and tires as well as the suspension itself, and it's important to consider all those variables and how those components interact with each other when making adjustments. A simple change—like a swap in tire size, brand, or even a

OPPOSITE: Take note of the brand, model, and size of your tires and any OEM variant suffixes that may follow the standard label. If you replace your tires with something different, be prepared to adjust your suspension to match. (ANDREW TREVITT)

different model in the same brand—can completely undo hours of work and testing.

Any setup is a compromise between a number of characteristics, and at some point you will have to make decisions as to your own riding style and what gives you the most confidence on your bike. When we make changes to a test bike's settings for *Sport Rider*, a lot of compromises are involved: We deal with riders ranging in weight from 130 to 190 pounds, skill levels from beginning motorcyclist to expert-level road racer, and styles from the classic smooth and tidy to ham-fisted and extreme. The ideal setup for a 140-pound novice rider is obviously going to be a lot different than that for a 200-pound expert-level racer, and that can make for a nightmare when trying to keep several riders sharing a bunch of bikes all happy.

You are more than likely not concerned with multiple bikes or riders and simply want to make your bike work its best for you—your particular weight, experience, and style. Even still, plan on encountering situations where a compromise must be made. If you like a nice soft ride on the freeway, you may have to put up with a bit of flightiness in the canyons. For quick steering, you may have to

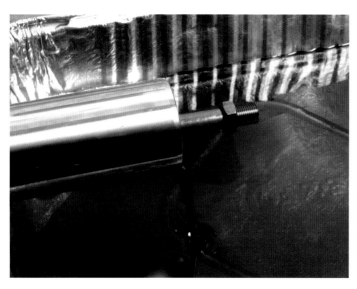

put up with some instability. Even the race track requires compromises, as every corner is different and your bike will work better in some turns than others. And, of course, your riding experience and style will change over time.

Before you start twiddling adjusters, it's important that your bike is in good working order. It's practically useless to try and change damping in a fork that is bent or has old fish oil (a derogatory term for the lightweight fork oil that was most likely in your bike when it was new). Likewise, there's no point in making adjustments for slow steering caused by an underinflated front tire, or trying to fix a wobble when your steering-head bearings are loose enough

to rattle like a baby's toy. Take the time now to go through your owner's manual and check the basic maintenance items. This will save you time and angst later. Obviously, it's important that your fork and shock are in good working order: Nothing is more frustrating than finding what feels like a good compression damping setting only to have your ride turn into a pogo stick a few miles down the road when the shock heats up. Leaky seals are a definite no-no, and if your bike has more than a few thousand miles on the odometer—some bikes are notorious for significantly degraded suspension performance in as little as 4,000 miles—consider some fresh fork oil and shock fluid. Racers especially should start with a known brand and weight of fork and shock fluid, change the fork oil every few races, and freshen the shock at least once a year.

Every component of a motorcycle's chassis plays a part in its handling, and slop or excess friction between those components can cause some real headaches. Using jack stands under the engine or frame, raise the front end off the ground—you want the wheel and fork unsupported for this inspection. Hold an axle clamp in each hand and gently rock the front end forward and back. A clicking noise is evidence of loose steering-head bearings. Remove your steering damper and let the front end flop from side to side.

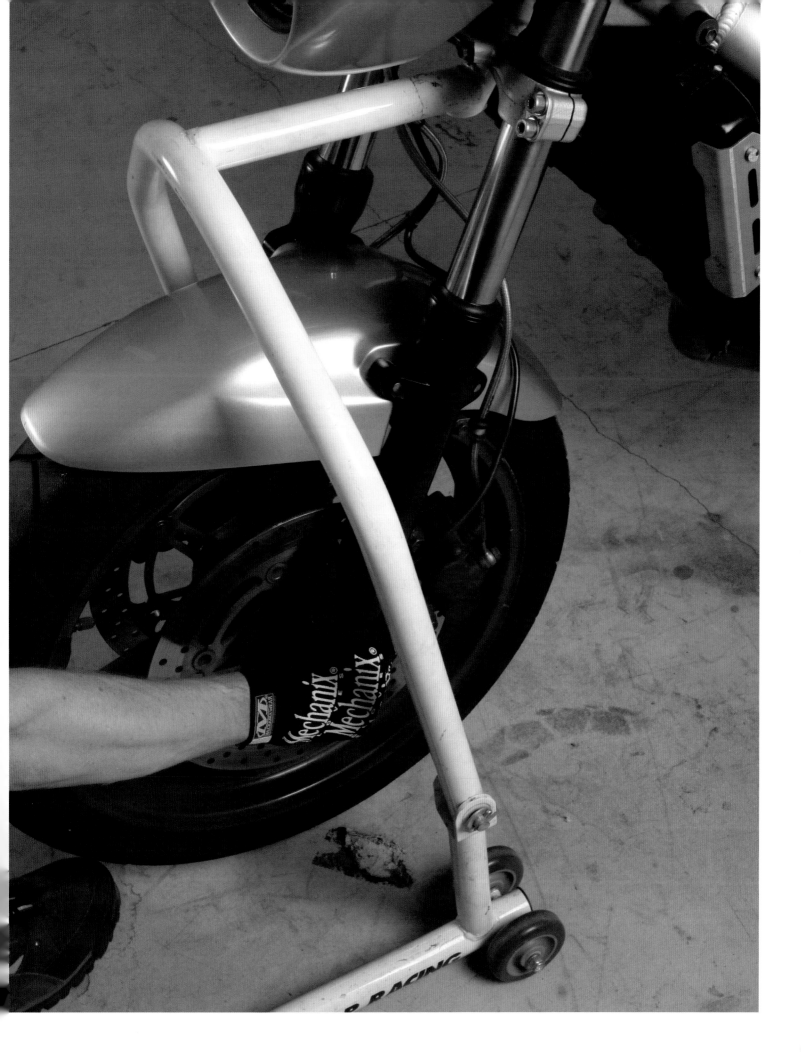

If it sticks or is difficult to move, the bearings may be too tight or worn. Adjust them according to the service manual for your particular bike. From the side, grab the top and bottom of the front wheel and try to rock it back and forth, feeling for looseness in the wheel bearings. Both wheels should spin freely, with little or no brake drag.

You'd be surprised at how much chain tension can affect your bike. A too-tight chain can literally freeze the rear swingarm under power by not allowing suspension to compress. Too much slack, on the other hand, can make for a jerky ride, unsettling your bike just when you want it the most stable—at the apex when you're trying to get on the gas. I generally err on the loose side, because it's a lot easier to deal with the jerky ride than it is to fight suspension problems caused by a too-tight chain. Check your manual for tension guidelines, and once you're happy with a certain amount of slack, find a point at which you can consistently measure it.

Because a rear shock's linkage is subject to all the dirt and water tossed up by the front tire, those bearings need attention every few thousand miles. Support your bike on footpeg stands or a jack, so that the rear wheel is off the ground. Check for any wear in the linkage and shock bearings by lifting the rear wheel—any play before you feel the shock's resistance is indicative of a worn bearing that should be replaced. Rock the rear wheel from side to side to check the condition of the swingarm pivot and bearings. Your service manual will detail the procedure to correctly torque the swingarm pivot to minimize play.

By far the most important consideration is tire choice and wear. In my earlier years of 250 racing, when my brother was tuning our TZ250S and we were both learning about its adjustable suspension, we would spend an entire practice day chasing a setup for a particular track—only to put fresh tires on for race day and have to start all over again. It took us a few events to learn not to pointlessly mess with the settings once the tires got beyond a certain point. Make sure your tires are in good shape before you begin, and know that if you change brands—or size, or model, or type—you may have to make some drastic changes to match. Set pressure to what the tire manufacturer recommends and check it regularly—every week on your street bike, morning and afternoon if you're at the track.

Your bike's tool kit should have all you need for basic adjustments: a flat-blade screwdriver for the damping clickers, a wrench for the front preload adjuster, and a C-wrench for the rear shock's preload collar. Most bikes' tool kits will have the C-wrench,

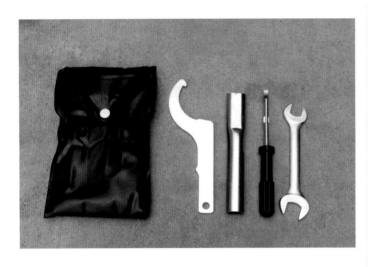

but if not, a trip to the salvage yard will most likely reward you with one for almost nothing. While those are fine to start with, better-quality tools will make the job easier. For example, when adjusting front preload, a 6-point socket will keep the finish nicer than an open-end wrench or 12-point socket. Specialized rear preload spanners are always better quality—the ends don't round off—and are easier to use because they tend to be longer and have more leverage. The downside, of course, is that the bigger tool is difficult to bring along on a ride. To make more-elaborate changes, you'll need a wider variety of tools. Each chapter details what you'll need to make adjustments related to that specific topic.

The most important tools, however, are a notepad and writing implement. Legible, orderly notes are paramount for keeping track of setups, whether for different tracks, tires, or roads, or as you gain more riding experience and require changes to your bike as you improve. Some riders and tuners prefer to use a notebook and keep everything in diary format; others use a standardized form for every race event, track day, or even individual practice session. Included in chapter 9 are some standardized setup sheet examples that you can photocopy, but as you gain experience you will find your own preferences for taking notes. How you record information is up to you, but the important thing is that every change and how it affected your bike is written down in some fashion.

If that sounds like a lot of work before we even put a tool to an adjuster, it is. But this effort beforehand will pay off when you find the right setup and are confident that it won't be all for naught when a fresh tire is put on or you discover a binding shock linkage. With that good setup and confidence, you can concentrate more on your riding, working toward the next level.

CHAPTER 3

Basic Principles and Theory

A ny suspension system can be broken down into two parts—a spring and a damper. Each is responsible for a different aspect of the system, and while they work together to give you a certain ride quality and performance, in many cases they can be considered two separate mechanisms.

SPRINGS

A spring's main characteristic is that it exerts an amount of force based on how far it is compressed. For example, a 1kg/mm spring (a common rate for a front fork spring) compressed by 1mm will exert 1kg of force. Compressed by 10mm, it will exert 10kg of force. You can also consider it the other way around: Set a 10kg block on top of the spring, and it will compress 10mm.

This linear relationship can be written as:

$$F = k * x$$

F = the force exerted, in kilograms or pounds

k = the spring constant, in kg/mm or lbs./in.

x = distance, in mm or inches

Most springs are linear—that is to say, the value of k is constant no matter how far it is compressed— but some are progressive and have a higher rate the more they are compressed. It's worth noting that "no matter how far it is compressed" applies only until the individual coils touch each other. At that point, the spring has reached coil bind and has an effective spring rate of infinity. You may have seen a shock with two springs installed in series; this is another way of varying the spring rate over travel. The softer of the two springs provides a low rate over the initial part of the travel. At a certain point, that spring becomes coil-bound and the second, stiffer spring takes over.

A spring's function is to support your bike's weight and allow the wheels to move relative to the rest of the bike over bumps. Ideally, when you ride over a bump the spring momentarily absorbs the force of the bump and allows the wheel to move vertically while the rest of the bike carries on without being disturbed. On the downside of the bump, the spring releases the energy it absorbed on the upside of the bump, pushing the wheel back down. In a perfect world the

OPPOSITE: A spring preload adjuster does not change the stiffness of the spring itself, but rather how much the spring is compressed initially. Changing the spring itself is the only way to change actual stiffness. (MARC COOK)

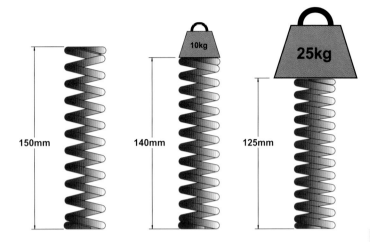

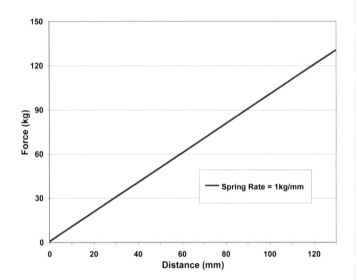

a worst-case scenario—where bumps in the road coincide with the suspension's movements—the oscillations may even become more and more pronounced over time if the driver doesn't change his speed. On a car with completely worn-out shocks, it's interesting to note that two natural frequencies are present: the slow oscillations of the car as it glides over rolling bumps, and the quick, stutter-bump action of the wheel itself over rough pavement.

Returning to motorcycles, one common misconception is that the preload adjuster on a fork or shock changes the stiffness of the spring. But a spring's rate cannot be changed; the spring itself must be replaced. Adjusting preload changes how much initial force is on the spring when the shock or fork is fully extended and, in turn, how far the shock or fork is compressed with a given load. We'll discuss how to set and adjust preload in detail in chapter 5.

DAMPING

To *damp* something, according to the Oxford English Dictionary, is to "take the force or vigor out." The damper, or shock absorber, slows the spring from compressing or extending too quickly, absorbing the energy of the movement and turning it into heat. The key to understanding damping is knowing that it controls the speed of the wheel's movement, whereas

tire would never leave the ground. Unfortunately, a spring alone cannot dissipate that energy—it can only store it temporarily and then release it. This brings about a natural frequency at which the spring likes to vibrate, or bounce. Once compressed it will extend, and then continue compressing and extending at that frequency—just like a Slinky toy.

This is seen in many everyday examples, with the most relevant for us being a car with worn-out shock absorbers. Even the smallest bump will start the car bouncing up and down, and it can take several iterations, or oscillations, before the car steadies. In

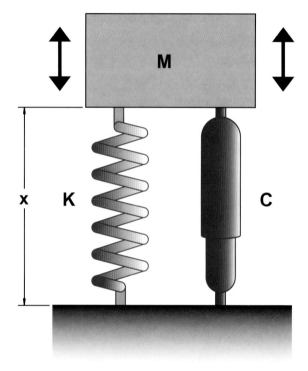

the spring controls the distance the wheel moves.

Because the wheel moves in two directions relative to the bike, we refer to—and in most cases can adjust—damping in both those directions. Compression damping controls how quickly the spring compresses, and rebound damping controls how quickly it can extend back to its original length. When you push down on your bike's suspension, the compression damping is at work. How fast the bike returns to where it started is dependent upon rebound damping.

Furthermore, in chapter 6 we'll consider both the high-speed and low-speed characteristics of damping, especially compression damping. Low-speed and high-speed refer not to the speed of your motorcycle as it travels down the road, but to the speed of the wheel as it moves vertically in relation to the rest of the bike. Some examples of low-speed compression damping are front-end dive while braking, or rear-end squat under acceleration—anything that moves the suspension relatively slowly through its travel. High-speed damping comes into play when you ride on the freeway over expansion joints, or over a sharp-edged bump that wants to compress the suspension quickly. In the last several years, more and more sportbikes have sprouted adjustments for both low- and high-speed compression damping.

RAKE

TRAIL

GEOMETRY

Your bike's chassis performance and its steering manners are largely determined by rake and trail, two critical dimensions of the front end. *Rake* is defined as the angle of the steering head relative to a line perpendicular to the ground and is usually between 20 and 25 degrees. On most bikes this is a fixed dimension, because the steering head is rigidly fixed to the frame. On others, such as Ducati's 999 series, rake is adjustable through inserts in the steering head. *Trail* refers to the dimension from where the steering axis intersects the ground to the center of the front tire's contact patch. Imagine a line drawn through the steering head, which in most cases is parallel to the fork tubes. That line will pass just behind the front axle and meet the ground a few inches in front of the tire's contact patch. The measurement from that point back to the contact patch (which is directly below the axle) is the trail. Trail is determined by—and can be calculated from—rake, the offset of the triple clamps, and tire diameter, and generally falls between 80mm and 110mm.

Trail provides a self-centering force to the front wheel, giving the motorcycle its stability. When the handlebar is turned, the tire's contact patch arcs to the side of the bike's centerline, slightly forward of its original position. The friction force of the tire

rolling over the ground constantly tries to push the tire to its rearmost position—in-line with the bike. In general, a steeper rake will give less trail, and this makes a bike steer quicker at the expense of stability. Sportbikes have relatively little trail for good handling, whereas cruisers have lots of trail for stability. While we may not be able to alter rake or trail directly, we can change rake—and, in turn, trail—slightly by raising or lowering one end of the bike relative to the other. On most stock bikes the only way to accomplish this is to raise or lower the fork tubes in the triple clamps, but some bikes have a ride-height adjuster incorporated into either the shock or the linkage to raise or lower the rear end. Ride heights and geometry are the subject of chapter 4.

Another important aspect of rear-end geometry to consider is the angle of the swingarm relative to the ground and frame. As bikes become more and more powerful, the engine exerts enough force on the rear suspension through the chain to affect geometry and handling. How this can be used to your advantage, by "tuning" the amount of force transmitted to the suspension and creating anti-squat, is explained in chapter 7.

Geometry and Ride Height

How a bike steers plays such an important part in its handling and setup that it can almost define a particular model. For instance, when we think of the early generations of Yamaha's R6, what comes to mind is an ultra-nimble middle-weight with laser-precise steering that borders on twitchy. That made for a dream ride on smooth pavement, but the little Yamaha could often become a handful on rough roads—more than once I sported bruised wrists thanks to a tank-slapping R6. Likewise, Ducatis have long been known for slower, heavier steering but rock-solid stability. As mentioned earlier, steering quickness generally comes at the expense of stability, and these two characteristics can leave a big impression on riders of all experience levels. For novice riders, easy steering is important to build confidence: A bike with light, neutral steering will allow a beginning rider to more easily learn good habits rather than constantly fighting his or her bike. Likewise, nothing will discourage a new rider

OPPOSITE: On most stock bikes, the only way to change geometry is by raising or lowering the fork tubes in the triple clamps. This directly changes the rake angle, and hence the trail. (COURTESY OF TRIUMPH)

more than a twitchy, unstable motorcycle that seems to have a mind of its own even when ridden in a straight line.

As you gain riding experience, you may find that you prefer a specific front-end feel. Perhaps you want quicker steering and have learned to use your body position or other inputs to limit instabilities in certain corners. Or you may grow to appreciate stability and feedback and be willing to work harder in fast transitions to turn your bike from side to side. You also should consider the differences between the street and the track: A setup that gives great steering characteristics and works fine in controlled conditions at the track could easily turn into a wobbling mess on a rain-grooved freeway.

The geometry of a particular model is generally defined by its rake and trail. We will discuss other critical dimensions in detail in later chapters, but rake and especially trail are the most important. Changing rake and trail can alter the steering characteristics of your bike. Those characteristics can most easily be classified in terms of steering quickness and stability. Steep geometry, with low rake and trail numbers, will give light, easy steering, especially at lower speeds. The trade-off for that quick steering is stability. With steep, aggressive geometry your bike may want to shake its head over bumps or when accelerating out of a turn. Relaxed geometry—high rake and trail numbers—generally results in heavier steering but more stability. At lower speeds especially, your bike will have a trucklike feel and be very reluctant to turn. Rake and trail affect other handling traits, but steering and stability are the two most important factors to consider when adjusting your suspension.

This is the first hands-on chapter in this book, not only because steering and stability are some of the first handling traits you should be making suspension changes for, but also because practically every adjustment you make will affect geometry and steering in some way. It's something you must always be aware of when working toward your ideal setup: even a small change to preload or damping can affect steering. Quite often riders will misinterpret the results of such a suspension change, crediting a new steering or stability character to what they adjusted rather than considering how geometry changed when they made that particular adjustment. That said, read through chapter 5—and make sure your bike's sag numbers are reasonable before making changes— so that you fully understand the important relationship between preload and geometry.

The easiest way to feel how your particular bike

reacts to a geometry change is to conduct a back-to-back test for yourself. This is a theme repeated throughout this book: Experimentation is the best way to find for yourself what a specific suspension change affects. At the race track, or on a quiet stretch of road that you are familiar with and represents the type of riding you do, make laps or passes until you are comfortable with the speed you are going and with how your bike is working. You should not ride at a pace that taxes your riding abilities, but rather at a speed that leaves you spare concentration to think about what your suspension is doing.

In this case, you want to experiment with changing rake and trail by adjusting ride height. Few sportbikes have provisions for adjusting geometry directly, but we can change effective rake by raising or lowering the front end of the motorcycle. This is accomplished by sliding the fork tubes up or down

in the triple clamps. Raising the tubes in the triple clamps lowers the front end, decreasing rake and trail numbers for steeper, more-aggressive geometry. Lowering the tubes in the clamps raises the front end, increasing rake and trail for more-relaxed geometry. See the sidebar on page 39 for a detailed explanation of how to adjust your fork tube height.

A change in fork tube height of 4mm generally equates to 1mm of trail, and experienced riders can easily feel that small of a change in geometry.

If your bike has a rear ride-height adjuster, it's easier to make quick changes using the adjuster rather than moving the forks in the triple clamps. Most aftermarket shocks have a threaded collar at the bottom of the shock, and this can be extended or shortened by loosening the lock nut and turning

the adjuster. Check the owner's manual for your bike or aftermarket shock for guidance. Many Ducatis have a rod in the rear suspension's linkage that can be lengthened or shortened to adjust ride height. Loosen both lock nuts—one is a reverse thread—and turn the rod to adjust the rod's length—again, your owner's manual will have detailed instructions and restrictions for the maximum length.

Extending the length of the shock or linkage will raise the rear end of the bike, decreasing rake and trail for steeper geometry. Shortening the shock or rod will lower the rear of the bike, increasing rake and trail for relaxed geometry. Because the magnitude of the actual change in ride height depends on the ratio of the linkage, you should make some measurements to find that ratio. With a friend lifting on the rear of

your bike, measure from the rear axle to a solid point on the subframe or seat directly above. Change the ride-height adjustment by one turn in the desired direction, and measure the change in rear ride height. In general, you'll find that a one-turn change equates to between 2mm and 4mm of ride height. As with the front end, a 4mm ride-height adjustment works out to roughly a 1mm change in trail. Experiment in one-turn increments, being careful not to exceed the maximum length specified for the adjuster.

Another possibility for altering rear ride height is to place a spacer between the top shock clevis and frame, effectively lengthening the shock and raising the rear end. Kawasaki offers a set of shims for most years of the ZX-6R and ZX-10R that slips in without requiring that the clevis be dropped completely from the frame, and the nut on the clevis is easily accessed. Aftermarket companies manufacture shims for Su-

zuki GSX-R models and Yamaha's R series. Recent Hondas, with their unique Unit Pro-Link setup, do not have a top frame mount or clevis, and hence, no provisions for an easy shim insert.

However you have decided to alter ride height, make a single change that sharpens your bike's geometry. That means lowering the front end by raising the fork tubes in the triple clamps by 4mm, extending the shock's ride-height adjuster by one turn, or adding a 1mm or 2mm shim under the shock's clevis—whichever is available or easiest for you to adjust. Certainly, raising the rear of the bike is not an identical adjustment to lowering the front, and in later chapters we will discuss the implications of each adjustment. If you are an experienced track-day rider or racer, you will want to experiment separately for raising and lowering the front separately from the rear. For most street riders and beginning track-day

ADJUSTING FORK TUBE HEIGHT

1 – Support your bike on a swingarm stand and, ideally, a front stand that supports your bike by locating in the steering stem. (MARC COOK)

2 – Measure from the top of the top triple clamp to the top of the fork tube itself. Most caps have rounded or unfinished edges, and the line marking the top of the tube is the most accurate reference point. (MARC COOK)

3 – On one side, loosen the top clamp's pinch bolt, the clip-on's pinch bolt, and then the bottom clamp's pinch bolts. (MARC COOK)

4 – Raise or lower the tube in the clamp the desired amount. It helps to have a friend to move the tube while you measure and then tighten the bottom pinch bolts. (MARC COOK)

5 – Torque the bottom pinch bolts to the value specified in your manual, then the top clamp and clip-on. Repeat the process for the other side, making sure both fork tubes are set to the same height. (MARC COOK)

6 – Never use a setup that requires you to have the tubes recessed in the top triple clamp, and always be sure you have enough clearance between the tire and the radiator, bottom triple clamp, and fairing—you can carefully remove both fork caps and let the bike settle on its suspension to check this clearance. Also check that your front brake lines have lots of slack with the fork fully extended. (MARC COOK)

7 – On bikes with inverted forks, make sure that you don't end up with the clip-on or either triple clamp pinching on a waisted portion of the tube. Be sure to check that your front end retains its full steering lock; it's easy to get an unpinned clip-on or a fork tube–mounted steering damper bracket out of adjustment, limiting travel in one direction. (MARC COOK)

8 – With conventional forks, check that the outer tubes don't touch the lower triple clamp before the tubes bottom internally. (MARC COOK)

riders, however, we are concentrating on the change in trail brought about by altering ride height. That change is far more apparent than the other effects of a ride-height adjustment, and for now you should just make whatever adjustment is easiest.

With the new setting, ride the same track or route as previously, at the same pace, so that you can concentrate on how your bike feels different. After the session, jot down your thoughts, detailing the setting change and describing how your bike reacted. Specifically, note any changes to stability and steering: Typically, sharpening geometry will make steering lighter at the expense of stability; the bike will be easier to turn, but may feel flighty or less stable. If you felt the change was for the better, experiment with another change in the same direction. If not, try adjusting ride height in the other direction.

Should you reach a point at which the fork tubes are flush with the top of the top triple clamp, don't be tempted to push the fork tubes down into the triple clamp. Likewise, don't go beyond the shock's adjustment limits or have the fork tubes extruded so far that the front tire is in danger of hitting the fairing or radiator at full compression. Note that it is possible to raise or lower the entire bike by raising or lowering the rear ride height and changing the fork tube height appropriately. This keeps rake and trail

the same, and you can use this to your advantage should you reach the end of an adjustment range. This also raises or lowers the center of gravity relative to the ground, and the troubleshooting guide found in chapter 12 outlines some scenarios where this particular adjustment could be useful.

We'll also look at how rake and trail are affected dynamically by damping and weight transfer. While the height of the fork tubes and the length of the shock set geometry with the fork and shock fully extended, your bike's rake and trail are constantly changing with every movement of the suspension. For example, under braking the fork is compressed and the shock is extended, significantly reducing rake and trail. How much the fork compresses and how far the shock extends in that circumstance—characteristics we can change by making other adjustments—will determine the dynamic geometry and how your bike behaves. For now, continue experimenting until you feel you've reached the best compromise of steering and stability for that particular road or track, and you are familiar with how a geometry adjustment—in either direction—changes how your bike feels.

5

Springs, Preload, and Sag

For all their simplicity, fork and shock springs have a big job to do—they are the only things holding your bike up, after all. We know from chapter 3 that a spring will compress an amount proportional to the weight or force it is subjected to; that relationship depends on the stiffness, or *k* value, of the spring. When you sit on your bike, the suspension compresses; add a passenger and it sinks even further. In addition to supporting the weight of you and your bike, springs also compress under cornering, braking, and acceleration forces. Maximum braking into a turn will transfer nearly all the weight to the front, sometimes lifting the rear wheel off the ground and bottoming the front fork. Likewise, hard acceleration will transfer weight to the back. Cornering forces can bottom both the front and rear suspension in extreme situations—this is a common occurrence around banked tracks like Daytona. The fork and shock springs must support all these constantly changing weights and forces, ideally without bottoming or topping out.

OPPOSITE: Make sure that your reference point for rear sag is a solid point on the subframe or seat, as directly as possible above the axle. (ANDREW TREVITT)

We can't change the rate of a spring without changing the spring itself, so there will always be some compromise in spring selection. However, your bike most likely has adjustments for front and rear preload, which can be used to change how the springs behave to a certain extent. *Preload* is a measure of how much a spring is mechanically compressed when the fork or shock is fully extended. For example, an extended fork tube may have a 300mm space inside for a spring. If we were to install a spring that is 315mm long, there would be 15mm of preload on the spring with the fork assembled. If that spring has a rate of 1kg/mm, the force it would exert on the tube is 15kg.

Now consider standing that fork tube up on the ground and pushing down on the fork cap. How much force would you have to apply to overcome the spring's preload? You'd have to push with an amount equal to that which the spring is pushing back—15kg—before the tube would compress. Now, turn in the preload adjuster by, say, 10mm to add more preload to the spring. In total, the spring is now compressed inside the tube by 25mm, and you would have to press on the tube with 25kg of force before it would move. In both cases, however, the

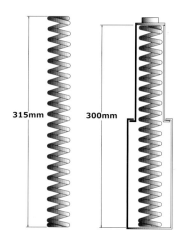

spring rate is the same—1kg/mm—and once the tube is compressed even a little bit, it takes 1kg of additional force to move it 1mm more.

The accompanying chart shows fork deflection vs. force for these two scenarios, as well as for a different spring rate of .9kg/mm. Note that changing preload makes more of a difference at small deflections, whereas a different spring rate shows up more with further travel. Consider, for example, if we were to add 10kg of force to our two imaginary fork tubes when they are near the top of their travel. The tube with the 1kg/mm spring would compress by 10mm, while the tube with the .9kg/mm spring would compress by 11.1mm—hardly a noticeable difference.

What if, however, we were to add 100kg of force to each tube? The 1kg/mm spring would compress 100mm, but the .9kg/mm spring would compress 111mm—a much greater change. In chapter 10, we'll look at spring rates and how the air gap inside the fork tube can also affect the suspension near the bottom of its travel. For now, it's important to realize that adjusting preload does little—if anything—to affect the actual stiffness of the suspension.

That being the case, then, just how *does* preload change the way the suspension works? Mostly, it is used to change the suspension's range of operation within the total travel available. With an ideal

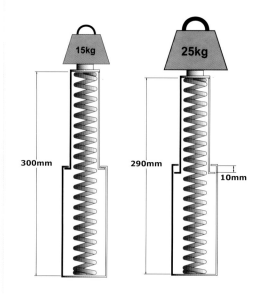

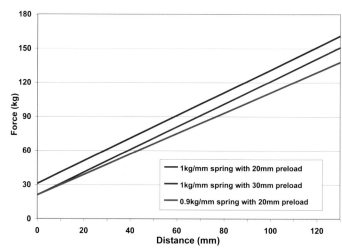

suspension setup, you want to use almost—but not quite—the full range of travel. On whatever track or roads you are riding, the front or rear suspension should not bottom out—compressing so much that the mechanical stop inside the fork or shock is reached—or top out—the fork or shock is fully extended. Topping or bottoming the suspension will cause a loss of traction and upset your bike every time it happens. Conveniently, most sportbikes are equipped with springs that are stiff enough that using all the travel is unlikely—you may end up using only 90mm of a fork that allows 120mm of travel if you are light, or 115mm if you are on the heavy side. We can use the preload adjuster to set the range of travel used within the suspension's full stroke so that the suspension is not topping or bottoming.

One indication of where in the suspension's range you are working is how much your bike's fork and shock compress when you sit on the seat. This gives a starting point for the suspension to work in either direction, whether it's compressing over bumps or extending over dips in the pavement. That starting point is commonly referred to as *sag*, or *rider sag*.

SETTING SAG AND ADJUSTING PRELOAD

Traditionally, *sag* is defined as the distance from full extension that the suspension compresses when you sit on your bike. To measure sag, I've always used the method recommended by Paul Thede of Race Tech. It requires some calculations and assistance from two friends, but it is an accurate and repeatable number.

To measure front sag, have your two friends lift the front of your bike by the clip-ons or handlebar. Measure the amount of exposed inner fork tube, whether it's between the slider and axle casting on an inverted fork, or the slider and bottom triple clamp on a conventional fork. Call this measurement L1. While one friend supports your bike from the rear, wear your usual gear and sit in a riding position. The other helper gently lifts the front of the bike, and lets it slowly settle on its suspension. Measure again, calling this L2. Gently push down on the front of the bike, and let it slowly rise up. Measure once more for L3. Taking these two measurements takes into account any *stiction*—sticky friction—in the fork tubes, and we will average the two numbers

when calculating sag.

A brief sidenote about friction: The difference between L2 and L3 is an indication of just how much friction exists in your suspension—the greater the difference, the more friction. In the fork, friction exists between the tubes, seals, and bushings as well as inside the cartridge. Likewise, in the shock there is friction between the seal and shaft, and, internally, the piston and body. In the rear suspension, the link-age and swingarm pivot bearings also add potential friction. If L3 - L2 is more than 25mm for the front end, or more than 5mm for the rear end, too much friction is present and it's worth investigating. We'll discuss friction more in the next chapter. Returning to preload and sag:

$$Sag = L1 - (L2 + L3)/2$$

Repeat for the rear end, with one helper holding the front fairing to steady the bike while the other takes the three measurements, using the distance from the axle directly up to a solid point on your bike's subframe or bodywork.

As a general guideline, rear sag should be be-tween 25mm and 30mm for the race track, 30mm to 35mm for street riding. If your measurement is out of that range, you'll need to adjust your preload accordingly—stiffer for less sag, softer for more.

Some bikes have a simple stepped-collar adjuster on the top or bottom, and your tool kit should have a C-wrench to turn the collar. The collar may be labeled with numbers, in which case you can write down the old and new settings. Otherwise, count the number of notches from the full-soft position and record that. On most Suzukis and Kawasakis, the shock has locking, threaded rings to change the setting. As a measure of preload, record the distance from the top of the threads to the top of the two rings. Use

LEFT: A typical front preload adjuster will have lines on the side. Turn the adjuster counterclockwise (more lines showing) for less preload, or clockwise (fewer lines showing) for more. (MARC COOK)

a C-wrench—or a hammer and punch—to loosen the lock ring and spin it up and out of the way. Mark one of the tabs on the bottom ring with a Sharpie, then tighten or loosen it in one-turn increments as needed. Don't forget to measure your setting after you lock the top ring in place. Check your owner's manual for additional guidance for either setup.

Some shocks have a remote hydraulic unit, such as those found on some sport-touring bikes or Öhlins aftermarket shocks. Check the shock's manual for guidance, or find something that you can accurately measure to record for your preload setting. As a last resort, have one of your buddies lift the rear end of your bike so that the shock is fully extended, and measure the overall length of the spring.

With your bike's rear sag set for your weight, a handy way to see if the rear spring rate is in the right range is to check what is called *free sag*. That is a measurement of how far the bike sinks on the suspension under its own weight—not with you on it. Take the same measurements as you did for rider sag, but measure L2 and L3 with no rider on the bike. This number is ideally between 5mm and 10mm. As a quick reference, you should be able to just lift up on the tail section and feel a small but noticeable movement. If the shock is topped out under the weight of the bike, you most likely had to crank in a lot

of preload to account for your weight. You should look into a stiffer spring for your bike. Conversely, if you've got a lot of free sag, you probably softened the preload for your lighter weight and may need a softer spring.

Not too long ago, the same guidelines for rear sag would have applied to front sag: between 25mm and 30mm for the race track, 30mm and 35mm for the street. In the last few years, however, more bikes have been equipped with top-out springs or extra sag in an effort to better keep the front wheel on the ground exiting corners—something that's getting harder and harder to accomplish as bikes get more powerful every year. Front rider sag can be as much as 50mm on some street bikes, and I usually just make sure that front sag is no less than 25mm for a race bike, no less than 30mm for a street bike. Below those numbers the fork is in danger of topping out on acceleration, a situation that not only hinders traction but also causes tankslappers as the wheel continuously contacts the ground.

The differences between street and track settings are to account for the different conditions encountered. On the track, cornering forces are higher and the suspension is likely to be compressed more under those forces, and more preload is required. For a more comfortable ride on the street, less preload is

LEFT: Rear preload adjusters with threaded collars may require patience and/or brute strength to set. Use a C-wrench to loosen the top collar, and turn the bottom collar in one-turn increments. Use a Sharpie to mark a portion of the lower ring to keep track of the number of turns. (ANDREW TREVITT)

BELOW AND BOTTOM: If a C-wrench doesn't fit properly, you can use a hammer and punch or this handy preload tool from Race Tech. (MARC COOK)

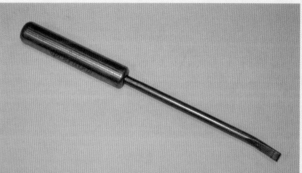

LEFT: Some sport-touring bikes, like this Honda ST1300, have a hydraulic adjuster that makes changing preload easy. The adjuster may have numbered lines to record the setting, or it may have a click-type adjustment. (COURTESY OF HONDA)

BELOW: This Öhlins shock has remote hydraulic preload adjustment. One way to measure preload is to count the number of turns from full stiff on the adjuster. I prefer to measure the gap between the adjuster's housing on the shock body and the spring collar, which is more accurate and easily repeatable. If you remove or change the spring, measure its installed length to be completely accurate, as the adjuster itself is movable. (COURTESY OF YAMAHA)

necessary so that the wheels can extend further into dips and potholes—the type of surfaces that aren't encountered on the track.

If your measurement for front sag falls out of the desired range, adjust your preload just as you did for the rear: stiffer for less sag, softer for more. Most bikes have a front preload adjuster incorporated into the fork cap—check your owner's manual for details about your bike specifically. Some adjusters will move in relation to the cap when you turn them, and you can record the number of lines showing on the adjuster as your measurement. Otherwise, turn the adjuster all the way in, clockwise, counting the number of turns until it lightly bottoms—that is the full-stiff position. Try not to slam the adjuster against its stop, but rather turn gently until you feel resistance at the end of the range. Make changes by turning the adjuster out more (softer) or fewer (harder) turns from full stiff.

Before riding your bike again, put a zip tie around an inner fork tube and snug it up so that it doesn't move on the tube. Slide it up against the outer tube's dust seal, and consider this a poor-man's data acqui-

sition system—the zip tie will indicate how much suspension travel you use in each riding session. You can keep track of this number, measuring from the zip tie to the axle casting on an inverted fork, or from the zip tie to the bottom triple clamp on a conventional fork. Don't forget to slide the zip tie back to the dust seal once you've taken the measurement after each session. Similarly, you can attach a small zip tie to the rear shock shaft, although it's more difficult to access and measure because of the spring and bump stop.

HOW PRELOAD RELATES TO GEOMETRY

Most riders consider sag and preload to be the first adjustments they should make on a sportbike, and you may have been wondering why the previous chapter covered geometry rather than beginning with springs and preload. That is because adjusting preload directly changes your bike's geometry, and it is important that you take this into consideration.

If you think back to the beginning of this chapter, you'll remember how preload affects only the initial force on the spring, based on how far the spring

is compressed inside the tube (or once mounted on a shock absorber). Say we have our imaginary fork tube from earlier in the chapter, still with a 1kg/mm spring and 25mm of preload adjusted in. Now, however, bolt a 50kg weight to the side of the tube, as shown in the diagram. How far is the fork tube compressed from full extension? Half of the 50kg weight goes toward overcoming the spring's 25mm of preload (25mm of preload on a 1kg/mm spring equals 25kg). The remaining 25kg compresses the tube an additional 25mm. What happens when we turn the preload adjuster in by 10mm? Now we have 35mm of preload on the spring, which takes 35kg of

the weight to overcome. Only 15kg of the weight goes to compressing the spring, meaning the fork tube will only compress 15mm instead of 25mm. The only change in the system is that the fork tube is compressed 10mm less than previously—exactly equal to the amount of preload that was added. Note that the top of the preload adjuster is exactly the same distance from the ground as it was before.

The fork tube reacts in the same way when it is bolted to a motorcycle: Adding 10mm of preload to the fork springs will raise the front of the bike by 10mm. As long as your suspension is not topped out or bottomed out, dialing in more preload does not

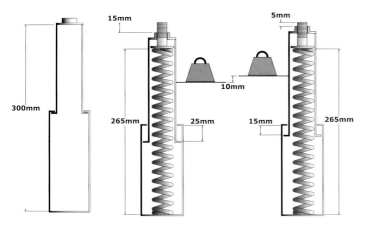

compress the spring more—it raises the bike on its suspension an equal amount, raising the ride height. Likewise, taking preload out lowers the bike on its suspension. Just as raising or lowering the fork tubes in the triple clamps changes geometry, adding or taking away preload also affects geometry.

Once you have set your sag to the proper range, experiment for yourself to find how preload and geometry are related. Just as you did in the last chapter, make a run with your bike as it is set up. Add or subtract four turns of front preload—about 4mm on most bikes—and ride again. You should notice that your bike reacted just as it did when you changed its geometry by adjusting fork tube height in the preceding chapter. Likewise, experiment with adding or taking away rear preload to raise or lower the rear end. Always remember to recheck your rider and free sag after making a change, and be sure to keep within the ranges recommended in this chapter.

Different road surfaces and types of race tracks will work your bike's suspension differently, and you can adjust your preload to better accommodate those surfaces. On a smooth and grippy race track, cornering forces will use more of the bike's suspension, and you can add preload to keep the fork or shock from bottoming—stiffer springs would also help. Add preload evenly front and rear, so

that the front and rear sag numbers change by the same amount. Conversely, a bumpy track will need more sag and less preload, as the wheels will need to extend into the dips and falling edges of larger bumps. In later chapters, we'll talk more in-depth about characteristics of forks, linkages, and shocks that also affect stiffness.

Damping

While preload adjustments make changes you can plainly see, turning a damping clicker has no visible effect—well, other than you can see the adjuster itself turn. Crank in rear preload, and you can watch the adjuster move on the shock body. Ditto on the fork in most cases, and you can watch either end rise or fall as you add or take out preload. However, turn a damping adjuster, and . . . nothing. Perhaps that is why people are even more reluctant to experiment with damping settings than they are with preload. More than likely, the real reason is that damping adjustments have a more subtle and dynamic effect than preload, and there are no measurements to make (such as checking sag for an indication of correct preload) to back up subjective riding impressions. Knowing exactly what happens when you turn that adjustment knob will go a long way toward demystifying damping, and by breaking down each setting into its components, we can address each one separately, simplifying the process.

DAMPING BASICS

There are many types of damping and equally many ways to achieve that damping. A twanging guitar string can be damped by a hand across the neck of the instrument, changing the sound. Electrical circuits have capacitors to provide damping. Skyscrapers sometimes have huge pendulum weights to control swaying in gusty winds. We are likewise concerned with controlling a particular oscillating motion—that of a spring—and that control is preferably supplied by oil flowing through passages.

Friction can also be used to supply damping, and in the early suspension days friction dampers were in fact used. Much like a windshield wiper on a car, a wiper was pressed and rotated against a plate to provide damping. My first race bike, the CB175, had a steering damper with this arrangement. It was even adjustable—crank down on a thumbscrew to put more force on the wiper, and you'd have more damping. Friction, however, is not one of the most consistent or reliable forms of damping, and eventually hydraulic dampers came into fashion. In

OPPOSITE: This '07 Suzuki GSX-R1000 offers both high-speed and low-speed compression adjustments. The low-speed adjuster is the screw in the center, while the high-speed adjuster is the larger nut. (COURTESY OF SUZUKI)

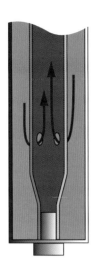

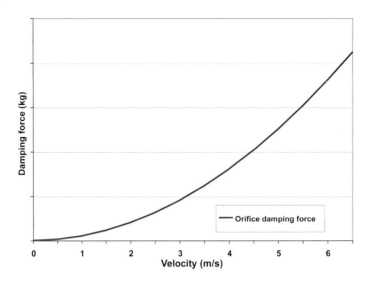

current-day suspension, we want the oil to provide *all* the damping, and we desire as little friction as possible to enter into the equation.

Thanks to people like Daniel Bernoulli, fluid dynamics is a well-understood field, and a precise level of damping can be achieved by forcing oil through an orifice of specific dimensions. In its simplest form, when a fork or shock is compressed, oil is forced through a hole of a certain diameter. The amount of resistance, or damping, depends mostly on three things: the viscosity of the oil, the size of the orifice, and the velocity of the oil. Put in thicker oil, and damping forces increase. Reduce the size of

the orifice, and force increases. Push the oil through faster, and force also increases. Because damping is related to the speed of the oil through its passage, damping forces depend on the *speed* of the fork or shock movement, whereas spring forces rely on the *position*, or length, of the spring itself.

Unfortunately, the force vs. velocity relationship is not linear, and this causes no end of frustration for manufacturers, suspension tuners, and riders. The relationship is almost the exact opposite of that desired in a fork or shock. The chart above shows how damping changes with the oil's velocity through a plain orifice—as the oil flows faster, force increases

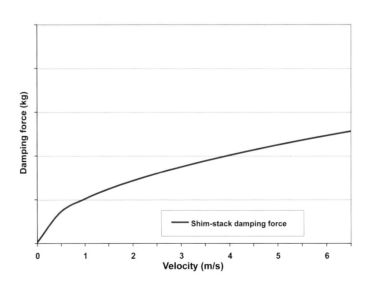

exponentially. Consider a tube of toothpaste or glue that you squeeze in order to force the paste through the opening—the orifice, in this case. If the opening were smaller or the paste thicker, you'd have to squeeze harder than normal to get the same amount out—that part is easily understood. But you've probably noticed how a light, slow squeeze will force the toothpaste out at a moderate rate. Squeeze harder, and the paste comes out faster. Squeeze harder again, and it comes out faster still, but not in proportion. Pretty soon you have to start squeezing awfully hard to force the toothpaste out faster, almost to the point that, no matter how hard you squeeze, it seems the toothpaste will come out only so fast. Of course, getting all that toothpaste back in the tube is another matter . . .

This is a common setup in older sportbikes that have damping-rod forks, and it works fine to a certain extent. For gentle, rolling bumps over which the suspension does not have to move quickly, there is little damping and the ride is comfortable. When you jump on the front brakes and the front end compresses, the harder you hit the brakes, and the faster the front end wants to collapse, the more damping is provided to arrest the movement—perfect. However, problems arise when sharp-edged bumps—hits in which we want the wheel to move a large distance in a short amount of time—are encountered. A prime example

would be running over a brick-shaped object in the road. In that case, we want very little damping to let the wheel move quickly up the face of the brick and not transfer that energy to the chassis. The nature of orifice damping provides an excess of resistance—so much that the fork can even lock up solid over big bumps, the exact opposite of what is desired.

This leads to the separation of damping into high-speed and low-speed components. The speed doesn't refer to the speed of the motorcycle as it travels along the road, but rather the velocity of the shock shaft or fork tube and the oil flowing through it. In general, one relationship of damping vs. velocity is desired for

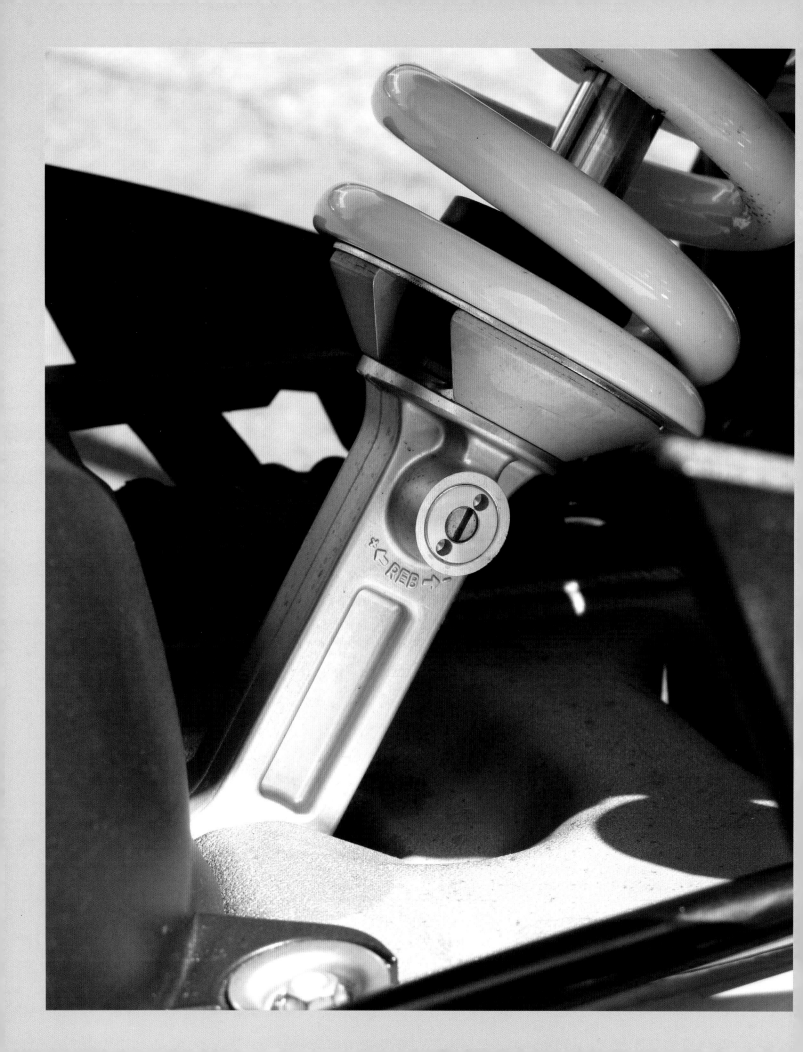

low-speed action and another for high-speed. How can this be accomplished? Consider again the tube of toothpaste or glue, but now put a larger opening with a cap that has a hinge and spring—much like the exhaust pipe of a big diesel truck or the tiny door your dog uses to get in and out of the house. If we squeeze the tube lightly, the cap opens very little, letting some toothpaste out. Squeeze harder and the cap will open further, providing a bigger orifice. Harder again, and the orifice gets even bigger. In this manner, the restriction provided by the velocity-squared curve can be nullified. By using a stiffer or lighter spring on the cap, we can provide almost any relationship of damping to velocity. This is almost exactly how a shock absorber or cartridge fork works—a larger-than-necessary opening, with shims providing the spring-and-cap effect to open the orifice a set amount for a given velocity.

COMPRESSION AND REBOUND

As mentioned in chapter 3, compression damping limits how quickly the fork or shock can react to a bump in the road that compresses the suspension. *Rebound damping*, or *tension damping*, is the opposite and limits how fast the wheel can return to its original position as the spring extends. It is beneficial to separate the compression and rebound damping

circuits, as a different amount of damping is required for each. Compression damping, dealing only with the deflection of the wheel and other parts that make up the unsprung weight, can be lighter than rebound damping, which must absorb the extending spring forces in addition to the heavier, sprung mass.

An example of a system with no damping is a pogo stick: Jump on the pogo stick to compress the spring, and with no damping it will extend back almost immediately. The result is both you and the pogo stick bouncing off the pavement. While that may be fun, a motorcycle that bounces off the road is not. When you hit a bump in the road, the wheel is deflected upward, compressing the suspension into the chassis. Too much compression damping will let the bump push the chassis itself upward, and you will feel the bump. Not enough compression damping will let the wheel bounce right off the road, just like the pogo stick. How much of each bump is transmitted through the suspension and to the rider determines how comfortable the ride is. And, of course, keeping the tire on the ground as much as possible is necessary for traction.

On the downside of the bump, rebound damping comes into play. Too much will allow the chassis to hold the wheel off the ground, and it will float off the top of the bump. Not enough rebound damping, and the suspension can push the wheel so hard into the ground that the chassis will be forced upward—maybe even enough to top out the suspension and lift the wheel off the ground. Just as with compression damping, rebound damping plays a large part in comfort and traction.

An ideal suspension system has just the right amount of damping to allow the wheel to track perfectly over both the leading and trailing edges of a bump. The compression damping would be light enough that the leading edge of the bump is not transmitted to the chassis, but firm enough that the wheel doesn't leave the ground at the top of the bump. Likewise, the rebound damping would be light enough to allow the wheel to track down the trailing edge, but not so light as to push the chassis upward. Sounds simple enough, in theory. But the trick is adjusting the damping settings to account for every type of bump and for any speed at which those bumps may be encountered.

In most shocks and cartridge forks, valves with shim stacks carry out the bulk of the damping. The number, thickness, and diameter of the shims provide the damping characteristics, and the valving can be changed to suit practically any condition. While revalving a fork or shock is discussed in chapter 11, we are more concerned with the external adjust-ments available to you. Most current sportbikes have rebound and compression adjusters on both the fork and the shock. A separate circuit for each diverts oil away from the main valve and through an orifice. The adjuster turns a tapered needle into or out of the orifice, changing its effective diameter. Turn the adjuster in—clockwise—and flow is restricted, adding damping and making the suspension stiffer. Turn the adjuster out—counterclockwise—for less damping to make the suspension softer. Because of the needle-and-seat arrangement, be careful to avoid overtightening the adjuster when turning it near the end of its adjustment range; you could damage the internals.

Currently, few sportbikes have high-speed rebound adjustment on the fork or shock, but more bikes are coming equipped with high-speed compression adjusters. A typical high-speed compression adjustment setup on a production sportbike consists of a shim covering a large orifice. A spring holds the shim closed, and at low shaft velocities oil flows only through a small bypass for low-speed damping. At higher shaft velocities, however, enough oil pressure is created that the shim is forced off its base, opening the main orifice and the high-speed damping circuit. Turning the high-speed adjuster in puts more preload on the spring that holds the shim closed, and more

ABOVE: On some shocks, the rebound adjuster is a knurled knob co-axial with the shaft at the bottom of the shock. (MARC COOK)

pressure—or shaft velocity—is required to open it. With this arrangement, typical of most stock suspension pieces, the high-speed adjuster only changes the crossover point at which the high-speed circuit is engaged. High-quality aftermarket parts have circuits designed such that the actual amount of high-speed compression damping is changed.

ADJUSTING REBOUND DAMPING

A fork or shock will naturally want to extend because of the spring forces involved, and the rebound circuit's duty is to dissipate that energy in a controlled fashion, keeping the suspension from extending too fast. Because the spring is a known quantity, and you can feel rebound damping working against the spring by simply pushing down on the bike, setting rebound is slightly easier than compression. I generally address the rebound damping adjustment first, because it's possible to achieve a decent setting without riding the bike. Additionally, the effects of a change in rebound adjustment are more readily apparent when you do ride the bike and, hence, easier to troubleshoot. Compression damping—especially on today's sportbikes that have both low- and high-speed settings—is slightly more of a fine-tuning adjustment: If your rebound setting is off, messing with the compression setting will have little effect on the overall handling of your bike.

The rebound adjusters on almost all sportbikes are in the same location. On the front fork, look for a screw on the very top of each fork leg co-axial with the larger preload adjuster. It may be labeled as REBOUND or, sometimes, TENSION. While most bikes have identical rebound adjusters atop each tube, some bikes (like the '06-generation Yamaha FZ1, '05-generation Triumph Speed Triple, Kawasaki Z1000, and many Moto Guzzis) have the rebound adjuster on one and the compression adjuster on the other. Check your owner's manual to be sure, and also to find the listed full range of adjustment. On the rear shock, the rebound adjuster is usually at the bottom, and it is either a cylindrical, knurled adjuster co-axial with the shock shaft or a small screw inset into the bottom body of the shock. Again, check your manual for the exact location and range of adjustment.

It's unlikely that your bike has separate high- and low-speed rebound adjusters on either the fork or the shock. One exception is the high-end MV Agusta F4 1000 models, which have a special Sachs shock with high- and low-speed adjustments for both compression and rebound damping. That case aside, OEM components and even the majority of aftermarket shocks and forks lack high-speed rebound adjustment. Certainly, experienced racers can take

advantage of tuning the rebound circuit by making internal modifications to the fork or shock, but such changes (and, likewise, any adjustments made to the MV Agusta's high-speed rebound clicker) are best made after consulting with a professional suspension tuner or aftermarket supplier. For the rest of us, the discussions in this chapter refer to the standard rebound damping adjuster.

Some adjusters have detents and make an audible and tactile click to help you keep track as you make a change—others do not. The settings are recorded in terms of the number of clicks or turns out from full stiff, whichever is appropriate. On your front fork, use a snug-fitting flat-head screwdriver to turn one of the adjusters in, clockwise, until it is lightly seated against its stop. Count either the number of turns or number of clicks as you go, and write that number down as the current setting for later reference. With the adjuster turned all the way in, it is now at its full-stiff setting. Repeat for the other adjuster; you should have to turn it the same number of turns or clicks to its stop—always keep the left and right fork settings identical. With the adjusters turned in to full stiff, take your bike off its stand, make sure the transmission is in neutral, and grab hold of the clip-ons or handlebar. With the front brake applied, give a firm shove on the front fork to compress the suspension as much as you can, and then release the force (without letting go of the clip-ons or front brake!) to let the front end rise on its own. Make a mental note of how long it takes for the fork to extend back to the starting point—it should have taken more than a couple of seconds with the rebound set to full stiff.

Next, carefully turn each rebound adjuster out to the softest setting, counting turns or clicks as you go. Continue until the adjusters lightly seat against their stops, and write down how many clicks or turns you made. This is the full range and should be close to what your manual says. It may not be exactly as listed due to tolerances in manufacturing and assembly, but it should be within a few clicks or one turn. Any more of a discrepancy may be an indication of something awry internally. With the adjusters in the full-soft position, push down on the front end just as you did earlier. Now it will most likely return much faster, and it may even overshoot the original position before settling back down. In some cases, the suspension may even oscillate for a couple of cycles before stopping.

With some bikes, there is an interaction between the compression and rebound circuits. Most often, this results in the compression damping feeling different after you make a change to the rebound adjuster, but sometimes it's the other way around.

Specific models that come to mind are the Kayaba forks on the '03 Kawasaki ZX-6R and the '03–'04 Suzuki GSX-R1000, and the Showa forks on some Buells. On those bikes, softening or stiffening the rebound damping can make a big, respective change to the compression circuit. If you do notice such a relationship between the two adjustments, keep this in mind when you make rebound changes.

Repeat the above sequence for the rear shock, by first turning the rebound adjuster in until it is lightly seated, counting turns or clicks on the way. Write this number down as your original, baseline setting. Have a friend hold the front of your bike while you stand behind and push firmly down on the passenger seat. Note how quickly the shock rebounds on the full-stiff setting. Just as you did for the front end, turn the shock's rebound adjuster all the way out, counting the full range of clicks or turns. Compare this number to what is listed in your manual. Push down on the passenger seat, and you should notice a similar change in action from full stiff to full soft as you did on the front fork.

A good baseline rebound damping setting is one that, after you push on the front or rear end, allows the bike to return to its original position in about one second. At a minimum, the suspension should not rise up beyond where you started and then settle back down—that is definitely too little damping. To find a baseline setting for your shock, turn the rebound adjuster in to one-half of its full range, and check how long it takes to rebound after a push on the passenger seat. If it seems too slow, soften the damping by turning the adjuster back out to approximately three-quarters of its range. If it's too fast, stiffen the damping by turning the adjuster in to one-quarter of the full range. Continue homing in on a good setting by halving the adjustment increment each time—for example, if the full range is twenty clicks, begin by turning the adjuster in ten clicks. From there, stiffen or soften the adjuster by five clicks, depending on what you felt. Then turn two or three clicks at a time until you reach what you feel is appropriate.

You may find that it's only the first turn or first few clicks from the full-stiff setting that provide any noticeable difference in feel, and this is not unusual. A typical damping adjuster consists of a tapered needle that bottoms against a seat, and the design of the taper may be steep enough that it need only be slightly off the seat for the circuit to be essentially wide open. Because of this, most damping adjusters are not linear—for example, a two-click change when the adjuster is close to full stiff will have much more effect than a two-click change when the adjuster is

more open. Keep this in mind when making changes, and always check the change you make by pushing on the fork or seat.

Getting back to our baseline setting, write down what you determined was an appropriate setting for the shock rebound as a number of clicks or turns from full stiff, then go through the whole process again with the front suspension. Aim for the same one-second interval for the forks to extend after a push, working in the same increments.

Compare the rebound settings you've reached using this method to what the original settings were; if you're more than a few clicks or a turn away on either adjuster, your bike will certainly feel different on the road. Now it's time to suit up and go for a ride to find out. Bring along your notebook and the tools necessary to adjust front and rear rebound damping. Use the same track or route as when you played with preload settings, and make a baseline run. If your bike feels different than it did before, write down what has changed and whether it's a positive or negative change. You can always go back to your original settings and make a second run to double-check what you're observing.

Rebound damping is responsible for some specific handling characteristics, and being aware of these traits will help you know which direction

to go when troubleshooting. In general, rebound damping will manifest itself over a series of bumps. As the suspension extends after the first bump, too-stiff rebound damping will not allow the wheel to return to its original position before the next bump tries to compress the suspension again. Over each successive bump, the fork or shock progressively compresses more and more and gets stiffer and stiffer—sometimes you can actually feel the bike getting lower as you go over the bumps. This is commonly known as *packing*, and you will feel this as the suspension gradually stiffens and compresses over the series of hits and the ride gets progressively harsher. Alternatively, if the rebound damping is too light, the suspension extends too quickly after the first bump, lifting the bike up. When the next bump is encountered, the suspension extends even more, further lifting the bike—sometimes to the point that the wheel is off the ground more often than on. This can lead to loss of traction, instability, and the feeling that the bike is "loose" or seems to be dancing over rough sections.

I usually gauge front rebound damping by how the bike responds to letting off the front brakes entering a corner. Experienced riders can trail brake deep into a corner to keep the front suspension perfectly compressed as the brakes are released

RIGHT: The shock's compression adjuster may be on a remote reservoir, as shown here. (MARC COOK)

BELOW RIGHT: The rear shock on this Yamaha YZF-R6 has separate adjustments for low-speed and high-speed compression damping on the reservoir at the top of the shock. Other bikes may have a screw-type adjuster for low-speed, with a co-axial nut for high-speed. (COURTESY OF YAMAHA)

ABOVE: The compression damping adjuster for the rear shock is typically at the top of the shock, on or near the reservoir. (MARC COOK)

OPPOSITE: When checking front damping with the bike stationary, hold the handlebar or clip-ons and apply the front brake. Press down with a firm push to compress the suspension as much as possible. Release the force, but not the front brake! (MARC COOK)

and cornering forces take over, but for the rest of us there is that moment (or two) between the time the brakes are let off and the bike takes a set in the corner. When front rebound damping is too light, the suspension will extend too quickly when the brakes are let off, and this will feel like a momentary loss of traction entering the turn as the wheel rebounds. Ideally, the rebound damping will be set to help you keep that front-end height and geometry constant entering a turn.

Out back, a sign of rear rebound damping is how the bike acts on the brakes in a straight line. As you brake, weight transfer compresses the front suspension and the back end will want to come off the ground. Having the rear rebound set too stiff can hold the back wheel in the air, or so that it is just skimming the pavement, leading to instability on the brakes—the rear end will wander from side to side.

With those symptoms in mind, now it's time to experiment. Decide on a change to make, and turn the appropriate rebound adjusters to a point that feels noticeably stiffer or softer when you push down and release the front or rear end. When making a change, I find it most beneficial to work in steps of one-third of the current setting. For example, if the rebound damping is at fifteen clicks out and feels too stiff, I

would soften it by five clicks to twenty clicks out. If the current setting is one and a half turns out, I would make a half-turn change. Make a run, and write down what you experienced and how you think your suspension behaved differently from the previous passes. If the change was for the better, continue further in the same direction, or work back and try the opposite direction. Even if your bike feels perfect, experiment with stiffer and softer rebound damping on both the front and rear ends. This process should give you a good idea of how too much and too little rebound damping feels. Continue to make changes from there based on what you've learned.

ADJUSTING COMPRESSION DAMPING

While it's possible to go through a similar process as we did for rebound damping to find a baseline compression damping setting, the changes are simply too subtle to properly feel just by pushing on the suspension. And, too often, what you feel in the pits or in your garage doesn't relate to how your bike will behave on the road or track. Compression damping is far too dependent on characteristics like unsprung weight, the construction and stiffness of the tire, and what kind of surface you are riding on—you won't feel any of that until you ride. For example, on a magazine project GSX-R1000, we installed carbon fiber wheels that were several pounds lighter than stock. To account for the huge drop in unsprung weight, we had to *increase* compression damping. The lighter wheels were deflecting more over bumps, and more damping was necessary to better control the lighter wheels. No amount of pushing on the bike in the pits would have shown a difference in that instance.

That said, experienced riders and suspension tuners can push on a bike and make changes to compression damping, based on personal preferences and a feel for what damping setting works well with certain combinations of bikes, modifications, riders, and tracks. When you push on the front or rear of the bike, the rebound damping works against the spring force—a known quantity—to push back. The compression damping resists only the force you put into the downward push, which changes from person to person, bike to bike, and surface to surface. People who can make a compression damping adjustment without riding a particular bike on a particular road or track are making those adjustments based on past experience and knowledge built up over time. There is no rule of thumb like there is for rebound damping that will help you here.

The compression damping adjusters on most forks are near the bottom of each tube, just above and behind the axle. Again, some machines have compression in one fork tube, rebound in the other; on those bikes, the adjusters are in the fork caps. Several models now have separate adjustments for high- and low-speed compression damping, and typically both will be located on a module bolted to the front of the lower fork tube. On the rear shock, the compression adjuster will be on the top of the shock body or on the reservoir, which may be integrated into the shock or on a hose and tucked away under the seat. Just as with the front fork, high-speed and low-speed adjustments may be separated. Check your owner's manual to see what adjustments you have available and their exact locations.

As mentioned previously, high-speed and low-speed damping does not refer to the speed you are traveling, but rather to the speed the fork or shock is being compressed. When you push down on your bike in the garage, that is the low-speed damping circuit. Front-end dive under braking is low-speed, as is rear-end squat under acceleration. A sharp bump in the road, such as the earlier-mentioned brick, a freeway expansion joint, or a Bott's dot, works the high-speed circuit. A section of rough pavement typical of a quick patch job is high-speed, almost regardless of how fast you ride over it. If your bike or aftermarket suspension component has any high-

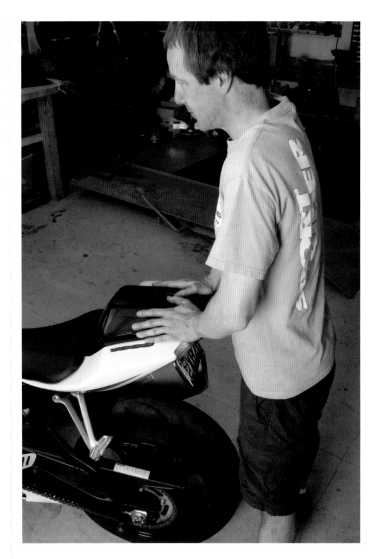

speed compression adjustments, set them to what your manual recommends for a start.

As you did for the rebound damping, turn the front low-speed compression adjusters in to their stiffest settings. Count the number of turns or clicks as you go, and be careful to lightly seat the adjuster to avoid damage to the internals. Make a note of the current settings, and check that the right and left fork adjustments are set identically. Grab hold of the clip-ons or handlebar, apply the front brake, and firmly push down on the front end. The fork should feel excessively stiff, and you should not be able to compress it very far no matter how hard you push. Set the adjusters to their softest position, noting the full range available, and again push down on the front end. Now the fork should feel significantly more plush, and you should be able to use up a lot of travel with a firm push.

Repeat this process for the rear end, adjusting the low-speed compression adjuster (on the reservoir or the top of the shock) to its stiffest and then softest position, and push on the passenger seat. Note the change in how hard you have to push to move the suspension the same distance each time and how each setting feels relative to how the front end felt at its softest and stiffest settings. Based on what you've learned so far, you should have an idea of what a

too-stiff or too-soft setting for compression damping feels like. Using that knowledge, return both the fork and the shock to their original low-speed compression settings, the midpoint of their adjustment ranges, or what your manual recommends—for now the actual setting is not critical, but rather that you've recorded everything and can refer back to those settings.

There is one final item to check in your garage, and that is how balanced the front and rear compression settings are. With your bike on level ground, stand to one side and place one hand on the rear of the tank—about where your sternum would go in a riding tuck—and the other hand on the front of the seat. Press down very firmly on the tank and seat, and note how each end compresses. Pushing in the middle of the bike, the front and rear should go down at a similar rate. If that's not the case, make adjustments until you feel the fork and shock are working in a balanced manner.

That done and all your baseline settings recorded, it's time to suit up and go back to your usual track or test loop and ride your bike—pen, notepad, and tool kit on board. There are some key items to be cognizant of when dealing with compression, and, as always, you should ride at a pace that leaves you concentration to spare. Make a run with your current settings to determine if any changes you made earlier have had an effect. Note how your bike felt over single hits as well as sections of rough pavement—both in terms of comfort and traction. Too much compression can make the ride harsh and rough, with the tires losing traction over bumps that could be absorbed better. Too little can cause the bike to wallow like a Cadillac over a series of bumps. As well, too little compression damping can have the wheels bouncing off bumps, again losing traction. These characteristics can be related to either high- or low-speed compression damping, and the trick is determining which to adjust. In general, big, single hits, such as a large, sharp-edged bump or a deep depression in the road, affect high-speed damping. Smaller bumps, or a series of bumps, are low-speed. It's worth noting again that the high-speed adjuster may have little effect, due to its design, and should be changed from the standard setting only when you've tried a low-speed adjustment first. Make single changes based on what you experience, keeping track of each adjustment and writing down your thoughts. As with rebound damping, I like to work in steps of one-third of the current setting to be sure of making a noticeable change.

How your bike works over bumps is half of the compression-damping equation. The other half is how compression damping affects geometry and ride height entering and exiting turns. Rake and trail are active dimensions, changing as you ride and affecting steering and stability. When you brake for a turn, the fork's compression damping controls how quickly the front end dives and how quickly the rake steepens. Likewise, when you accelerate out of a turn, compression damping in the shock determines geometry and weight transfer. How quickly the fork dives under heavy braking is a good indicator of front low-speed compression damping. The front end should compress smoothly and at a modest rate through its travel, reaching equilibrium just at the point of maximum braking. With too little compression damping, the fork will blow through its stroke, possibly to its stop, and then rise up slightly. Too much damping and the front will ride high through much of the braking zone, resulting in reduced feedback and traction. Keep an eye on the zip tie you wrapped around a fork tube earlier—it should show between 5mm and 15mm of travel left after each session.

Similarly, rear-end squat characteristics can be altered with low-speed compression damping. While we'll address squat in much more detail in chapter 7, one option to control weight transfer on corner exits is to adjust rear compression damping. Too much squat can cause the front end to get light under acceleration and your bike to run wide. Alternatively,

not enough squat can hurt rear traction exiting a turn. Add or remove damping to find a setting where you have a good compromise between the two.

That's a lot of symptoms to keep straight while you ride, and it's easy to become overloaded when dealing with compression damping. Even experienced riders can have difficulty with this aspect of suspension as they attempt to juggle the characteristics it affects. For most of us, the important part is to at least experiment enough to find settings we are comfortable with. With that comfort comes confidence, which equates to safety on the street, speed on the track.

Squat and Anti-Squat

One aspect of suspension and handling that is becoming more prominent as bikes get more powerful every year is squat and anti-squat under acceleration. Just as weight transfer works to compress the front suspension as you brake for a corner, weight transfer under acceleration puts more load on the rear of the bike, compressing the rear suspension. This is commonly referred to as *squat*. Conveniently, due to the geometry of the swingarm, sprockets, and chain, the force in the chain can be used to counteract that weight transfer. This force, which extends the rear suspension, is generally known as *anti-squat*. Ideally, when you exit a corner the squat and anti-squat forces will offset each other in such a way that your bike gets the optimum combination of rear traction for acceleration and front traction for steering. As we shall see, finding that balance is a hard task, especially with a heavy and powerful bike.

OPPOSITE: Using small front sprockets exposes the danger of having the chain running directly on the top of the swingarm at the pivot. Under acceleration, the taut chain can literally pull the pivot down, compressing the rear suspension. Always check for sufficient clearance when using a smaller-than-stock front sprocket. (ANDREW TREVITT)

You are most likely familiar with weight transfer under acceleration. In the most extreme situation, a wheelie will transfer 100 percent of a bike's weight to the rear wheel. The anti-squat geometry and characteristics that virtually all motorcycles possess are not quite so well understood. However, once you grasp how swingarm angle, sprocket selection, and swingarm pivot height (if your bike has such an adjustment) can be juggled to use that anti-squat to your advantage, your motorcycle's handling can be significantly improved with some slight changes.

Grit your teeth now because we have to—briefly—dig back into high-school geometry to properly study anti-squat and its effects. Two forces combine to provide anti-squat. The first force is the road pushing on the rear tire as you accelerate out of a corner. Remember that for every action (the tire pushing on the ground to accelerate), there is an equal and opposite reaction (the ground pushing back). This force is referred to as the *driving force*, and if the swingarm slopes down from its pivot to the axle—as it does in almost every motorcycle—the driving force will act to extend the suspension as you accelerate. You can see this in action by putting your front wheel against a building or solid object and carefully applying some throttle and gradually releasing the clutch—without making the rear tire spin, mind you. As you apply power to the rear tire, the rear of the bike will rise up, enough so that the suspension can completely top out.

The second force involved is the chain pull. The power of the bike's engine, fed through the chain and sprockets, pulls the rear wheel in the direction of the top chain run—toward the engine. Almost every chain-driven motorcycle has a small front sprocket and larger rear sprocket, and this creates a force that will try to extend the rear suspension. The two forces—driving force and chain pull—can be calculated and combined to find a total force that can be used to offset squat. Bikes with shaft drive have a different set of forces to deal with, which typically result in too much anti-squat. Manufacturers use various methods to decrease or nullify the effect, such as the BMW layout (shown on pages 4 and 5) that employs a parallelogram arrangement. The options for tuning anti-squat in these cases are severely restricted, but on a chain-drive bike the forces can be manipulated by changing sprockets. It all sounds simple enough—simply pick sprockets and swingarm angle so that the resultant forces all cancel each other out, right? Not so fast . . .

In some ways, the squat/anti-squat problem all

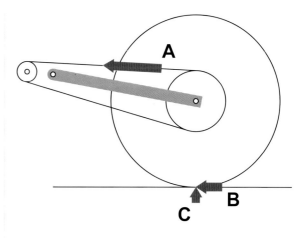

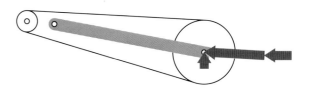

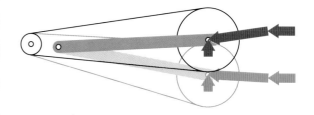

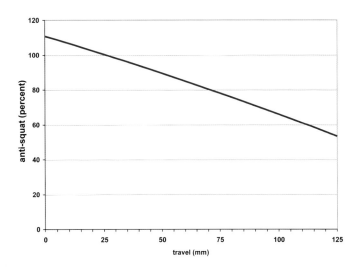

works out nicely. As you feed more power to the rear wheel, there is more weight transfer, which results in more squat. However, more power is also being fed through the chain and to the rear wheel, and chain pull and driving force will increase proportionately. This means that under any amount of acceleration, the anti-squat characteristics are close to the same in relation to the squat characteristics. The problem, though, is that as your suspension compresses, the relationship between the swingarm and chain run changes. The swingarm angle flattens out and may even go negative. And because the front sprocket is in front of the swingarm pivot, the angle between the swingarm and chain also changes. This alters the direction of the forces involved, changing their sum and hence the amount of anti-squat. Not only that, but the traditional layout used on every sportbike causes the anti-squat force to *decrease* as the suspension compresses—exactly the opposite of what you want to counteract squat!

This is what drives tuners and riders, especially those dealing with powerful race bikes such as superbikes or 1000cc superstock machinery, to pull their hair out. The "sweet spot," where the forces all work out and squat is nicely offset with anti-squat, is found in only a small range of the suspension's travel. If the rear suspension is extended beyond that point, there is too much anti-squat, and the suspension will stay extended, not letting weight transfer to the rear tire for good traction. If the rear suspension is compressed too much, decreasing anti-squat will lead the suspension to compress even more, unloading the front end. And the relationships all change depending on how much traction is available at a certain track or in certain conditions.

Too much squat, or too much anti-squat, will manifest itself fairly clearly, especially on a bigger bike. Sometimes you will be able to literally feel the rear of the bike raise or lower as you dial on the power out of a turn, especially at the extreme of one or the other. Most likely, however, you will have to watch for other, more subtle symptoms. One sign of too much anti-squat—not enough weight transfer—is simply poor traction under power. When the rear tire starts to spin even moderately exiting a corner, the squat side of the equation loses its effect and the chain pull forces take over. The swingarm extends, stepping the rear wheel out and worsening an already-bad situation. In an extreme case, this will all happen so suddenly that the wheel can seem to snap sideways as the rear suspension extends suddenly.

At the other end of the spectrum, not enough anti-squat—too much weight transfer—is characterized by a flighty front end on rough corner exits as the fork tops out over the bumps. Even on smooth pavement,

too much squat can cause understeer, giving your bike a tendency to run wide under power.

How can we change anti-squat characteristics? As a rule of thumb, the greater the angle between the top chain run and the swingarm and the closer the chain is to the swingarm, the more anti-squat you will have. To increase anti-squat for less weight transfer, you can:

- Increase swingarm angle by adding rear ride height or increasing rear preload
- Increase chain angle by making the front sprocket smaller or the rear sprocket bigger
- Raise the swingarm pivot, so that it is closer to the chain run

To decrease anti-squat for more weight transfer, you can:

- Decrease swingarm angle by lowering rear ride height or reducing rear preload
- Decrease chain angle by making the front sprocket bigger or the rear sprocket smaller
- Lower the swingarm pivot

Keep in mind two things when juggling these parameters to change anti-squat: First, small front sprockets can rob power by forcing the chain to curl too tightly and can also allow the chain to rub on the swingarm right at the pivot. This can completely nullify any setup changes, as the chain—should it run right on the swingarm—can pull the pivot down under acceleration. Always be sure that you've got some clearance on the top chain run. Second, changing gearing will have little effect on anti-squat if the actual ratio is not changed—for example, changing from a 15/45 setup to a 16/48 combination. Yes, the chain is further away from the pivot and this reduces anti-squat, but the new sprockets put the chain at more of an angle, increasing anti-squat almost exactly enough to offset the increased distance.

Notice that if you raise or lower the rear end to change anti-squat characteristics, you will also change the geometry of the front end, which may create a problem in other areas. One solution when raising or lowering the rear end to change the swingarm angle is to raise or lower the fork tubes in the triple clamps an equal amount, to keep the overall attitude of the bike the same. This will help retain the ideal front-end geometry you worked so hard to attain. Another is to use damping to control weight transfer and the squat characteristics, rather than making a geometry adjustment. More rear compression damping will decrease weight transfer under acceleration, while less compression will increase weight transfer and squat—again, this may have consequences elsewhere. Try to isolate the exact setup problem you are having, and make changes accordingly to least affect other aspects of your setup.

Tires

Tires are not generally considered part of a motorcycle's suspension, but they play a crucial role in your bike's handling. Many a rider has spent hours chasing a setup by changing preload, damping, and geometry settings and then promptly found all that hard work to be for naught when new tires were fitted. Set your bike's spring and damping rates way too stiff, and it's possible for the tires to end up as its *only* suspension, wearing the tires out prematurely and costing you money as well as wasted effort. And you've probably experienced how much a change in tire size or brand can change a bike's handling.

Sportbikes can (and, in fact, are expected to) work with tires from a huge selection of manufacturers and categories. A rider racking up most of his or her miles commuting or taking trips may fit a sport-touring tire for longevity. Someone hitting the canyons more often may fit the same bike with a set of sport tires, or even some hybrid street/track tires to attend track days regularly. Others will use DOT race tires or slicks for track days or racing. Not only do all these various types of tires have extremely different characteristics, but also each tire manufacturer's design and construction for a particular category is subtly different. This broad range of tires can require an equally broad range of suspension settings. Add the effects of different compounds, tire pressure, and wear on top of that, and you can see how easy it is to work in circles if you don't consider tires part of the overall equation.

The applicable tires for a sportbike can typically be grouped into five categories: sport-touring, sport, high-performance sport, DOT race, and slick. Sport-touring tires, such as Dunlop's D220, are intended for piling on mileage under heavy loads and over varying road surfaces. To last as long as they do, sport-touring tires are typically heavier than average, with more rubber for extended life and a stronger construction with more plies to support the weight of a heavy bike, a passenger, and luggage. Sport tires, the category into which most OEM tires fit, cover the widest spectrum of potential usage and offer a compromise of mileage and performance.

OPPOSITE: The range of sportbike tires includes (from top to bottom), racing slicks, DOT race tires, high-performance sport, sport, and sport-touring tires. Note the amount of tread siping on each, which particularly determines how well the tire works in the rain. (ANDREW TREVITT)

Bridgestone's BT-015, which comes as standard equipment on several models, is an example of a typical sport tire.

High-performance sport tires, such as the Michelin Pilot Power 2CT, are intended for both street and track use. These tires are also sometimes called *hybrids*, and the category is increasing in popularity as more riders attend track days. Typically, a given manufacturer's high-performance sport tire will be a combination of its sport-tire construction and race-tire rubber compound, or the opposite—the race-tire construction with a stiffer tread compound. In Michelin's case, the 2CT is similar to the standard Pilot Power, but with softer rubber on the edges of the tread. This gives better grip when the bike is leaned over, while retaining the standard tire's longevity. At the sticky end of the street-legal spectrum, pure DOT race tires such as Pirelli's Diablo Supercorsa are intended specifically for the track, and they wear the DOT label only to be eligible for production-based racing in many series. Expect minimum life and maximum performance from these bubblegum tires. Finally, slicks are also meant for the track only, with no tread siping for use in the rain.

When dealing with a chassis setup, consistency in tire selection is a priority. There's no point in even trying to make adjustments with one set of tires fitted if you're planning on swapping to a different brand or size for the next track day or ride. Too many variables are involved in each tire's profile, compound, and construction that affect how a bike works, and you'll only frustrate yourself by constantly changing to a different tire. Decide what compromise in mileage and performance (and budget!) you are willing to make, and then pick the appropriate category. Most

LEFT: Check the owner's manual or on the swingarm for tire-pressure recommendations for street use. At the race track, ask the tire vendor what pressures to use at that particular track. (ANDREW TREVITT)

BELOW: Most current sportbikes have a variant of a standard tire fitted as original equipment. For example, this 2007 Honda CBR1000RR sports Bridgestone BT-015F G and BT-015R G front and rear tires, indicating they are a "G" derivative of the standard BT-015. The setup required for the standard version of tire may be slightly different than for the variant. (ANDREW TREVITT)

riders err on the side of performance, insisting on DOT race tires for track days and even street use, but just in the last few years sport tires have closed the gap on race tires in terms of grip and have even *exceeded* their performance in some areas. Today's sport tires are easily capable of handling a track day and will provide much more consistent grip over a longer period of time than a race tire or slick.

New bikes are often shod with an OEM variant of a particular sport tire. For example, beginning with the 2007 model year, most Buell models are equipped with Pirelli Diablo T tires, which are subtly different in construction from the standard Diablo. The same is true of other tire brands on many sportbikes, with the specific tires labeled with an additional letter following the standard listing. The motorcycle and tire manufacturers work together in these cases; sometimes the desire is to enhance a particular characteristic of the bike, and sometimes the goal is simply to have a distinctive tread pattern. Should you replace an OEM-specific tire with the standard version—for example, replacing the Diablo T with a standard Diablo on a Buell Firebolt—there may or may not be setup ramifications. Check your tires for the additional labeling, and be aware of any tire variants available for your bike if you decide to stay with the original brand and model of tire.

When straying from the standard tires, there are many characteristics to consider when choosing a tire category. Obviously, switching to a sport-touring tire from a sport tire will sacrifice traction for extended mileage. But while you'd expect sport-touring tires to have a plush freeway ride, their stiffer construction and thicker tread can make them harsher than regular sport tires. Changing from a standard sport tire to a DOT race tire, which has incredible levels of grip, typically compromises stability to attain that traction. You may find with that switch that the only way to retain a good compromise between quick steering and stability is to fit a steering damper if your bike doesn't

ADJUSTING RIDE HEIGHTS TO ACCOUNT FOR CHANGING TIRE SIZES

Once you've made the decision to swap tires to a different size, brand, or model, you can ease the transition by measuring the old and new tires to find if any changes in ride height are necessary. Although you may be replacing your tires with new tires of the same size according to the numbers on the sidewall, subtle differences in the profiles can add up to big changes in how your bike handles. For example, a new front tire with a taller profile will raise the front of the bike, adding trail and slowing steering. Likewise, a new, taller rear tire will raise the rear end, sharpening the steering and possibly reducing stability.

Before the old tires come off, measure and record their circumferences as $C_{old\ front}$ and $C_{old\ rear}$. Use a thin retractable tape measure, or preferably a cloth tailor's tape measure, and circle the tire at its highest point. Likewise, once the new tires are mounted, measure and record the circumferences as $C_{new\ front}$ and $C_{new\ rear}$. The change in ride height necessary to account for the new profile is equal to the change in radius between the new and old tires. At the front end, the difference is calculated as:

$$\Delta RH = \frac{(C_{new\ front} - C_{old\ front})}{6.28}$$

The ΔRH is the distance the fork tubes should be raised in the triple clamps. A negative result indicates the new tire is smaller than the old, and the tubes should be dropped in the triple clamps by that amount.

Likewise, calculate the change in rear ride height as:

$$\Delta RH = \frac{(C_{old\ rear} - C_{new\ rear})}{6.28}$$

Here, ΔRH is the distance the rear end should be raised, measured from the axle up to a point on the subframe or bodywork. A negative result indicates the rear end should be lowered by that amount. Should your bike not be equipped with a rear ride-height adjuster, you can make the adjustment at the front end to at least get the correct attitude to the geometry. In this case, add the two results together:

$$\Delta RH = \frac{(C_{old\ rear} - C_{new\ rear}) + (C_{new\ front} - C_{old\ front})}{6.28}$$

Raise the fork tubes in the triple clamps by the calculated total; lower the tubes if the result is negative. Be sure to check all the clearances as outlined in chapter 4 when changing fork tube height.

It's doubtful you'll notice a change in ride height of less than 2mm or 3mm unless you're a racer with several years of experience; if the new tires are that close in circumference, it's not worth making a change that small without riding the bike first. While simply changing ride heights will not account for all the potential differences in the new tires' construction and profile, it will be a step in the right direction.

1 — Use a thin tape measure or tailor's tape to find the circumference of the new and old tires. (MARC COOK)

2 — Calculate the change in front and rear ride heights necessary to account for the differences in circumference. (MARC COOK)

3 — Adjust the fork tube height appropriately to account for the change in front tire height, or for both tires if your bike doesn't have a rear ride-height adjuster. (MARC COOK)

4 — Measure from the rear axle up when making a rear ride-height change in this case, not the change in the adjuster itself. (MARC COOK)

come equipped with one. Additionally, whereas sport tires will work on a variety of road surfaces and tracks with little or no adjustments, you'll most likely find your setup changes for each different track or type of road you ride with stickier tires fitted. Finally, race tires are intended to be used with tire warmers, and as such are not designed to warm up to operating temperature quickly—something to think about if you plan on using race tires on the street or attending a track day when the weather is cool.

Once you've chosen a category, ask other riders that own your make and model of bike for recommendations on what brand to use; oftentimes a particular bike will respond to certain tires better than others, and you should take advantage of other riders' experiences. In addition to price, you should also consider availability: Remember, you'll need a reliable, consistent supply, and getting a great deal on a single set of tires won't help you in the long run. Tire manufacturers are ramping up their presence at track days, with local vendors often providing support and fitment services, and this should be one of your considerations if you plan on going to the track often.

Tire pressure is often a hot topic of discussion, with as many different viewpoints as there are brands and models of sport tires. The easiest way to find the correct tire pressure for track use is to ask the ap-propriate vendor—either at the track or before you go—for the numbers. Only the top percentage of riders will be able to gain any benefit from changing tire pressures from those suggested numbers; if you start experimenting there is a good chance you'll make a change in the wrong direction and prematurely wear out a set of tires. Make an effort to find the right pressures before you leave for the track, and stick with those numbers—it will save you a lot of anxiety once you're there. Typically, pressures for the track are significantly lower than those recommended in your owner's manual for street use. For example, with grip as the prime issue in the controlled conditions of the circuit, wear and stability take a backseat, and pressures are set for optimum traction rather than all-around performance.

For street riding, you could utilize those low-track pressures for maximum grip, but there are trade-offs to consider. With less air in the tire to support the carcass, stability is decreased at lower pressures, especially in a straight line or at high speed. The additional flex that reduced pressure allows can overheat a rear tire, leading not only to increased wear but also to the chance of a failure. If you don't think street riding works a tire all that much, put your hand on your back tire after a long freeway stint—you may be surprised. The owner's manual for your bike will give you a starting point for pressure, with values most likely much higher than the pressures a vendor would recommend at a race track. Every bike and tire combination is different, and on the street, optimum tire pressure is more dependent on load and conditions. For example, the manual for Yamaha's 2007 YZF-R6 calls for a tire pressure of 36 psi in both the front and rear for loads of up to 198 pounds, and 36-front/42-rear for more than a 198-pound load. But for "high-speed riding," 36-front/36-rear is listed. The optimum street pressure is usually in between the track pressures—favoring grip—and the numbers in the owner's manual, which are based on more realistic loads and potentially extreme conditions. Ask around to see what other riders with similar setups are using for tire pressure, or start with the manual's recommendations and work down from there, taking notes just as you would when conducting any suspension change.

A tire's overall performance—and how that specific tire works with a specific bike—is determined by a huge number of factors. Without an unlimited budget to conduct your own testing to find the exact best tire for your bike, take advantage of what's available to you in terms of information. Talk to other riders and racers with the same bike about their findings with respect to what tires they've used, tire pressure, wear, and so on. Tire vendors at the track will take the time to talk to you about your needs and suggest a size, compound, and pressure based on hundreds of other similar setups and years of experience. Most important, resist the temptation to change to a different brand or size of tire if your overall setup isn't working. Sometimes it's an easy fix and your bike will work better with a different tire; more often than not, however, it's the first step down a frustrating and expensive trail. It's a lot cheaper to do your homework first and then spend some time to get your bike to work with a specific tire, rather than spooning on random tires in hopes of stumbling on a match.

CHAPTER 9

Finding a Setup with Stock Components

Up to this point, we've covered the various adjustments you can make to a motorcycle's stock components with basic hand tools. If you've experimented with each adjustment along the way, you'll have a good idea of how making those individual adjustments can affect handling. Finding a good setup or solving a handling malady, however, is rarely as easy as making a single change. Every adjustment—whether it's preload, ride height, or damping—has a domino effect that must be considered. For example, if your fork is topping out and skittering over bumps when you exit a turn, one remedy is to decrease preload to better settle the suspension. But preload also affects ride height, and decreasing front preload may take away enough trail to cause instability on the straight. A powerful bike, sensitive to swingarm angle, could develop too much anti-squat with that small change and spin too easily under power. Being able to juggle the different adjustments to make a specific change to the chassis's behavior is the challenge you face to find that optimal setup.

Late-model sportbikes are designed to accommodate a huge range of riders, varying in skill, weight, and riding style. The setup that makes a 200-pound beginner comfortable for his first street ride may be very different from that required for a 150-pound rider on the track. Stock components—with some fiddling—are for the most part capable of suiting those extremes to a reasonable degree. That capability does come with a price, however: In some cases, just a few clicks or half-turns can transform your bike from a nice-handling, comfortable ride to a bucking beast that's difficult just to hang on to. With that in mind, and taking into account the increasing number of adjustments available on the latest sportbikes—with exponentially more paths to wander down—it makes sense to take advantage of other people's experiences with a particular bike. More trackside vendors are offering suspension services, and for a nominal fee you can have an expert provide you with a baseline setting for your bike that is based on

OPPOSITE: If you can reach between the spring coils to put a small zip tie on the shock shaft, you can also check rear wheel travel. The zip tie may disappear inside the bumper if you're using close to maximum travel; carefully reach in with a Popsicle stick or other wooden or plastic item (so as not to damage the shaft) to push the zip tie up after every check. (ANDREW TREVITT)

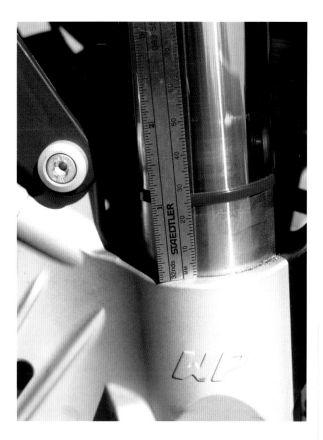

years of experience with countless numbers of similar bikes at dozens of tracks. In *Sport Rider* road tests, suggested suspension settings are listed that are based on feedback from a variety of test riders spanning a range of abilities and weights. After reading and conducting the experiments in the earlier chapters, you may already have made changes based on measurements you took or how your bike reacted to the incremental changes, giving you a baseline of your own to start with. Whether it's your current setup, a friend's settings that you'd like to copy, a setup taken from a magazine, or a baseline provided trackside, there are two important points to consider. One is to carefully record your baseline settings, so if changes you make aren't to your liking you can easily go back to where you were. The other is that if you're happy with the new setup, why stop there?

Race Tech founder Paul Thede, one of the most knowledgeable suspension experts in the country, has a favorite saying that has served me well since I first attended one of his seminars in 1999: "The best you've ridden is the best you know." Say you try someone else's settings on your bike and they work great; it's a comfortable ride, steering is quick, and you have better traction than previously. If you don't make changes from that point, how will you ever know that your bike could work even better? The bottom line is that it doesn't matter where you start from, you can always make, or attempt to make, an improvement from there. Likewise, you should never feel that you've found a "perfect setup" and stop experimenting. There will always be a different road or track, new tires, improved skills—any number of parameters that can benefit from different settings.

Once you've decided on a baseline, write everything down so that you can easily revert to that baseline should you go astray. There are multiple methods of tracking changes, from keeping notes in diary format to writing down every setting for each outing, whether it's on the street or track. On the one hand, working backwards through a plain notebook to find old information can be frustrating (especially if your handwriting is like mine!), and on the other, recording every setting for every session can be quite tedious. An in-between option is a single sheet for each day's riding, listing the initial and final settings, with the remainder in notebook format. At the end of this chapter are sample setup sheets, covering

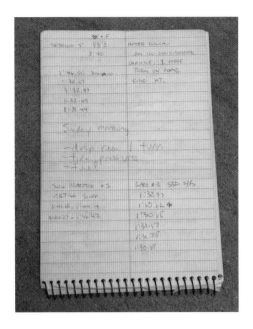

RIGHT: How you keep track of the changes you make is up to you. Some people use a diary format; others prefer to write down every setting for every session. The important part is that you can easily refer back to those notes and repeat a complete setup for any given day or track session. (ANDREW TREVITT)

all three options, that you can photocopy and use. They may be too extensive or not elaborate enough for you, but it's easy to make your own setup sheets in a spreadsheet program; use a system that is easy to adhere to, yet lets you quickly find data from any given outing.

When setting out to improve your bike's handling by making suspension adjustments, it helps to have a definite goal in mind. Identify a specific problem that you would like to remedy, such as the example at the beginning of this chapter, or work toward improving one aspect of the chassis you think could be better—without sacrificing handling in any other areas, of course. Setting out to simply play with your suspension and randomly tweaking things in the hopes of stumbling on an improvement rarely results in any gains and more often ends up in frustration. Work in single steps from your baseline, and avoid making multiple adjustments. In the example used earlier, the most evident course of action is to try the preload change, see how the bike is affected, and work from there. With more experience you'll be able to anticipate that the preload change may require an additional ride-height adjustment to remedy the specific characteristic outlined. At some future point you'll have the confidence to identify the problem and make those two changes at the same time.

When dealing with a new or unknown bike, I will rarely make adjustments prior to riding the machine, but will check several things beforehand (in addition to the usual pre-ride safety and condition checks). Once you've selected your baseline and set the adjusters accordingly, you should run through these checks as well. As outlined in chapter 5, check rear free sag by having a friend hold the bike while you lift up on the tail section. Between 5mm and 10mm is ideal, and if you've got too much or too little, you've already got one area to address after you ride the bike. Likewise, measure front sag (rider sag, with you on the bike), and ensure that it's more than 25mm for the track, 30mm for the street. Again, if you've got too little, that will be one of the first things to change after a ride. A couple of pushes on the front and rear of the machine will give you an idea of the rebound damping, as discussed in chapter 6. Note that depending on weather conditions, this may change significantly as the fork and shock warm up, and checking after the ride will show just how much the damping is affected. Finally, wrap zip ties around a fork tube and the shock shaft if you are able to reach in between the coils of the spring. This budget data-acquisition system will measure travel and reveal any bottoming.

As in the earlier chapters, ride your bike on a

road or track that is typical of your usual outings. Gradually up your pace until you find something that makes you uncomfortable or causes a loss of confidence in your bike's handling. Chapter 12 includes a troubleshooting guide that lists various handling symptoms along with suggestions for adjustments. Use this or the knowledge you gained by experimenting with each adjustment individually in the earlier chapters to help you pinpoint what made you uncomfortable. The first step to improving your setup is to identify a fault, then choose a possible solution based on all your experience. With time, it will become easier to find the problems as well as correct them.

The pre-ride check may have given you a good indication of what direction to go, and you'd be surprised at how often that is the case. Typically, a magazine test bike will arrive with loads of free sag in the rear shock—easily more than 10mm. A quick ride will reveal that steering could be quicker and the front end could be better planted. Knowing that free sag is on the excessive side, the easy fix is to add rear preload to put the rear free sag in the correct range. The preload change alters geometry enough to sharpen the steering, and knowing the numbers beforehand makes a decision easy. Likewise, knowing that a damping clicker is near the end

of its range of adjustment can guide you toward an avenue of experimentation.

In general, the first changes to make from a baseline setup are ride height and preload, with the goal of finding a good compromise between steering and stability. A balanced chassis will steer quickly and be stable on the straights, and the fork and shock will not bottom or top out. To find this balance on a stock bike, you will have to adjust fork tube height and preload at both ends to find the best combination. Find the right chassis angle (which determines rake and trail) first, which is best accomplished by raising or lowering the fork tubes in the triple clamps if your bike doesn't have a rear ride-height adjuster. Your current settings could also guide you toward making a different change to alter geometry: Let's say you'd like slower steering, which can be accomplished by lowering the fork tubes in the triple clamps to raise the front end and relax the geometry. But if the fork tubes are already flush in the triple clamps, that is not an option. That means that to make the geometry more conservative, you have to reduce rear preload to lower the rear of the bike, or add front preload to raise the front end. Furthermore, let's say that front sag is at 40mm and rear sag measures 35mm. You certainly don't want to reduce preload at either end with that amount of sag, so the natural adjustment would be to add some front preload. Adding 5mm of front preload would put sag to 35mm, which is still a safe and conservative number. Having everything written down and easily accessible really helps in these cases, and a lot of times the answer will present itself. Juggling the numbers and different settings may sound overwhelming at first, but it won't take you long to make these decisions once you're familiar with your bike and its components. Believe me, looking after one bike is easy once you've tried to sort out six bikes simultaneously for a huge comparison test!

When dealing with big bikes, keep in mind that squat will also be a factor, and one way to influence squat is to raise or lower both ends of the bike an equal amount by adjusting both ride heights or preloads. This changes the swingarm angle, affecting squat properties but keeping geometry consistent. Work toward finding a combination of ride heights and preloads in which the chassis attitude is good for steering and stability and your sag numbers are in the proper range. Once you've settled on the geometry, then the damping adjustments can be addressed. It's much easier to fine-tune for comfort and traction with a balanced chassis than to try and find decent damping settings when the bike is not settled due to incorrect geometry. As mentioned in chapter 6, work with rebound damping first, then compression, using the troubleshooting guide in chapter 12 for direction.

After each change, a number of options are available. Obviously, if overall handling is worse, you can revert back to the original setting, trying a similar adjustment but in the opposite direction (or even something entirely different). A definite improvement may lead you to make a further change in the same direction, but with successively smaller steps. The fun really starts when your bike is better in some ways after an adjustment, but worse in others. For instance, it could be that your bike steers better after a geometry change, but is less stable; alternately, it may be improved in some turns on the track, but worse in others. It's up to you to decide what characteristic or turn is more important and to make the next adjustments accordingly.

SETUP AND TIMING

Track: _____   Date: _____   Event: _____

1	_____	11	_____	21	_____
2	_____	12	_____	22	_____
3	_____	13	_____	23	_____
4	_____	14	_____	24	_____
5	_____	15	_____	25	_____
6	_____	16	_____	26	_____
7	_____	17	_____	27	_____
8	_____	18	_____	28	_____
9	_____	19	_____	29	_____
10	_____	20	_____	30	_____

New for this session

Changes during session

To do after session

Comments

SETUP AND TIMING

Track: _____ Date: _____ Event: _____

	Front	Rear
Ride height		
Preload		
Rebound		
HS compression		
LS compression		
Fork oil		
Oil level		
Spring rate		
Rider sag		
Free sag		
Tire size/compound		
Tire pressure		
Gearing		
_____		
_____		
_____		
_____		
_____		

Notes

Lap times

1	_____
2	_____
3	_____
4	_____
5	_____
6	_____
7	_____
8	_____
9	_____
10	_____
11	_____
12	_____
13	_____
14	_____
15	_____
16	_____
17	_____
18	_____
19	_____
20	_____
21	_____
22	_____
23	_____
24	_____
25	_____
26	_____
27	_____
28	_____
29	_____
30	_____

SETUP AND TIMING

Track: _____ Date: _____ Event: _____

	Initial settings		Final settings	
	Front	Rear	Front	Rear
Ride height				
Preload				
Rebound				
HS compression				
LS compression				
Fork oil				
Oil level				
Spring rate				
Rider sag				
Free sag				
Tire size/compound				
Tire pressure				
Gearing				
_____				
_____				
_____				
_____				
_____				

Notes

CHAPTER 10

Springs, Fork Oil, Fork Oil Height, and Other Mild Modifications

As capable as modern sportbikes are of handling a huge range of riding styles, rider weights, pavement surfaces, and conditions, some situations still call for getting our hands dirty. Covered in this chapter are some low-cost changes you can make that may help when you find yourself at the maximum or minimum of an adjustment range and desire more or less of that particular adjustment. Even if you aren't maxed out on any particular setting, just being aware that these options are available makes it easier at times to experiment down a particular setup path; you'll have these tricks in your back pocket to use if necessary. While the usual preload, damping, and ride-height adjustments can be made with simple hand tools and a moderate mechanical ability, these mild modifications may require special tools, a service manual, and more in-depth wrenching talent. That said, the work is easily executed once you have the knowledge and proper tools, and it's well worth understanding how the changes can affect your bike's handling.

SHOCK CLEVIS SHIM

As mentioned previously, most sportbikes lack rear ride-height adjustment, leaving us only the option of raising or lowering the fork tubes in the triple clamps, or using preload, to change geometry. Not only is moving the fork tubes a time-consuming job, but also clearance issues arise should you venture too far from the stock dimensions. On many models, the top shock mount is a separate clevis that fits through a hole in the frame and is attached with a large nut. Shims can be used between the clevis and the frame, effectively lengthening the shock and raising the rear of the bike.

Raising the rear end in this manner is a simple way to steepen the geometry of the bike without lowering the front end enough to cause clearance problems. You can also use a shim in conjunction with raising the front ride height to change swingarm angle without affecting the geometry. Or you may want to experiment with raising or lowering the whole bike on its suspension. Once you have some shims and the ability to adjust ride height out back, you can explore a number of

OPPOSITE: Instead of disassembling the fork tube each time you want to add or remove fluid, it's possible to make that change without a lot of work. Carefully undo the fork cap and let the upper tube slide all the way down. (MARC COOK)

ABOVE: Danger zone: When the zip tie indicates all or most of the fork travel is being used, adding a small amount of fork oil will help stop the fork from bottoming, with little effect on other handling characteristics. (ANDREW TREVITT)

BELOW: When a fork compresses, the volume of air inside decreases accordingly. In turn, increasing air pressure creates a force in addition to the spring force, effectively raising the spring rate as the fork compresses. (ANDREW TREVITT)

BOTTOM: When air is compressed, the resulting force increases exponentially, leading to what can be a steep increase in spring force. The shape of the curve near full compression can be changed by varying the amount of air in the fork tubes. (ANDREW TREVITT)

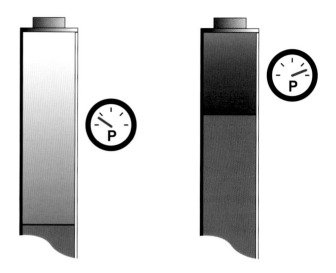

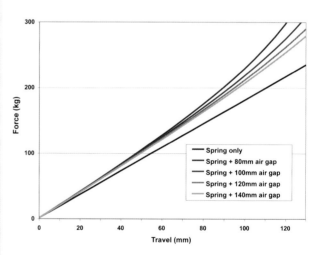

avenues. Several aftermarket companies offer sets of shims in various thicknesses, and Kawasaki has a kit with open-ended shims that can be slipped into place without removing the clevis completely. You could also measure the clevis and open area around it and head to your local hardware store to find a washer to fit. McMaster-Carr (www.mcmaster.com) has a good selection of large shims, some of which are even slotted. Keep in mind that the actual change in ride height will be between two and three times the thickness of the shim, due to the linkage ratio.

FORK OIL HEIGHT

When you change fork oil (you did put fresh fluid in your forks before we began, right?), your manual lists a measurement for how much fluid to put in each tube, either in terms of volume or a distance from the top of the tube. How much fork oil you pour in

determines the volume of air inside the fork when the spring is installed and it is all buttoned up. When the fork is compressed, that volume decreases, putting the trapped air under pressure. In turn, that pressure acts on the cross-sectional area of the fork to create a force that supplements the fork spring, resisting the tube's compression.

Unfortunately, we have to delve into a brief physics lesson again. From the ideal gas law, we

BELOW: Slip the shim over the clevis, and reinstall the clevis and top shock mount. Lower the rear end and tighten the large nut and the shock mount. Remeasure the ride-height reference to determine the actual change, and correlate that to the thickness of the shim. (MARC COOK)

BOTTOM: Torque the large nut to the specification listed in your service manual, and double-check the change in ride height with the shim in place. (MARC COOK)

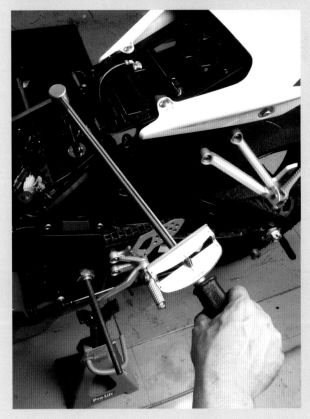

TOP: To add a shim under the shock clevis, begin by supporting your bike on jack stands and loosening the large nut. You may have to lift up the tank to accomplish this. Measure from the axle up to a fixed point for a ride-height reference. (MARC COOK)

ABOVE: With the Kawasaki shim kit, all you have to do is loosen the clevis nut enough to slip the shim into place. If you're using a washer, completely remove the nut and raise the bike enough that the clevis is free from the frame and you can install the shim. On some bikes, it's easiest to unbolt the top shock mount from the clevis rather than jack the bike up too far. (MARC COOK)

know that pressure doubles every time the volume is halved, leading to an exponential relationship. Likewise, the additional force created from the trapped air will increase exponentially as the fork is compressed. At the top of the fork's travel, the volume is large enough that the additional force from the air has very little effect. As travel is used up, however, the pressure increases and quickly comes into play. The graph on page 106 shows the relationship between total spring force and travel. A mechanical spring exerts a force proportional to travel (a linear relationship), and adding the exponentially growing force from the air pressure gives a total force that is only affected by the air pressure close to the bottom of the fork's travel.

This increasing force works as a convenient anti-bottoming device, which can be "tuned" by varying the amount of air trapped in the forks. Raising the fork oil height—leaving less air—will increase the effect close to the bottom of the fork's travel. Likewise, lowering the height decreases the effect—as shown in the graph. The most common scenario in which you would change fork oil height is when you are bottoming the fork under heavy braking. For instance, say you're happy with the way your bike handles and steers aside from the bottoming-under-braking problem, and you have good sag numbers.

One way to stop the fork bottoming is to increase preload, but there will be a change in geometry as a minimum penalty. Instead, adding a small amount of fork oil will increase the effective spring rate just at the bottom of the travel, where it is most needed, keeping the fork from bottoming on the brakes. A 10mm change in oil height is a good increment to work with, which generally works out to adding about a tablespoon's worth of fluid.

Likewise, you may find that your fork is *too* progressive near the bottom of its stroke, indicated by the zip tie on the tube and also by a lack of front-end feel under braking. One avenue to explore in this situation is removing some fork fluid, which will provide a more linear rate near maximum travel. Again, work in increments of 10mm height, or about one tablespoon of fluid. Your service manual will specify a standard value for fork oil height, as well as a range you should stay within.

SPRINGS

As mentioned in the previous chapter, most current sportbikes are capable of accommodating a wide range of riders, and this capability extends to front and rear spring rates. In my experience, many stock bikes are sprung suitably for a rider weighing between 145 and 165 pounds, but with some adjustments can

BELOW LEFT: Calculate a volume of fluid based on a desired height adjustment. For most forks, between 10cc and 15cc—or about a tablespoon—of fluid works out to 10mm in height. To add fluid, simply measure out an appropriate amount and pour it between the tube and the spring. (ANDREW TREVITT)

BELOW RIGHT: To remove fluid, it may be possible to use a syringe and a thin piece of tubing. Snake the tubing between the spring's coils and down into the fork tube. Draw out fluid until the syringe is about half full. Squeeze out the desired amount of fork oil into a pan. Reinsert the tubing and return the remainder of the fluid back to the fork. Button everything up and record the change you made in your notes. (MARC COOK)

BELOW: While many sportbikes have stock springs that work well for a surprisingly wide range of rider weight and ability, aftermarket shock or fork springs, with rates tailored specifically to your weight and riding style, can make an improvement. Most vendors will help you choose new spring rates based on your specific needs, and it won't be necessary to have a cart of springs on-hand like the race teams do at the track, as shown here. On damping-rod forks, swapping springs is a fairly easy process; changing springs on a shock or cartridge fork requires some patience and special tools. (RILES/NELSON)

be made to work well for riders weighing as much as 190 pounds, or as little as 130 pounds. Progressive springs and linkages help provide this range, as do other mechanical and valving tricks inside the fork tubes and shock. Not every bike offers this adaptability; some models are too stiff for riders at the lighter end of the range, while others are too soft for heavier folks. Still, riders weighing in the range of 130 to 190 pounds should be able to find a workable setup with the stock springs for moderate-to-aggressive street riding and the occasional track day. Outside of that range, or if you plan on going to the track on a regular basis, you may want to consider some alternate springs.

In chapter 5 we touched on how to determine if a rear spring is too soft or too stiff. To recap, the relationship between sag and free sag is a good indication of spring rate. With rear preload set to provide the desired amount of sag (25mm for track, 30mm for street), free sag—how much the rear end sags under its own weight—should be between 5mm and 10mm. Too much free sag is an indication that the spring is too stiff for your weight. While this may seem counterintuitive, consider what the measurements indicate: The more free sag there is, the less the spring is compressing when you add your weight—hence, the spring is too stiff. The less free

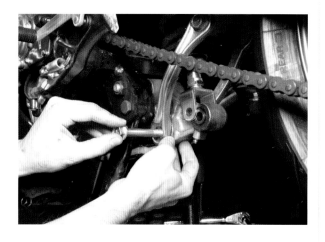

sag, the more the spring is compressing under the addition of your weight alone, meaning the spring is too soft.

Note also that this method indicates that a stiffer spring is recommended for the race track as compared to that necessary for the street. Say you have the recommended 30mm of sag for street riding with 8mm of free sag. Tightening up the preload to change sag to 25mm for the track will likewise decrease free sag a few millimeters, certainly to less than the ideal 5mm. To achieve the sag/free sag relationship for the race track in this case, a stiffer spring would be necessary. That said, it's important to realize that you don't have to rush out and buy new springs just to attend a track day. Most riders will be able to find a stock-spring setup that will work

fine on the track. In the example given above, you could add some rear preload so that sag is closer to 25mm, but not so much preload that free sag ends up being less than 5mm. As always, try to reach a compromise in the measurements and settings, and continue to experiment.

Changing a rear spring requires removing the shock and, in many cases, a spring compressor. As a guide, if your shock has threaded rings for preload adjustment, chances are good that you can unthread the rings far enough to easily remove the spring. On a shock with a ramp-type adjuster, count on using a spring compressor. Using jack stands under the footpegs or a frame stand, support your bike so that the rear suspension will be free to move and the rear wheel is just off the ground. Loosen the top and bottom shock mount bolts, and, while a friend supports the weight of the rear wheel, remove the bolts. Let the wheel drop gently to the ground, and remove the shock. You may have to remove some of the suspension linkage to successfully maneuver the shock out; your service manual will detail the complete procedure. With the shock removed, measure and make note of the installed length of the spring. Use a spring compressor to remove the old spring and install the new one, or take your shock to a shop that can do the swap for you—don't attempt to jury-rig

something to do it yourself. Reinstall the shock, and set the sag accordingly.

Up front, it can sometimes be less clear that a spring is too stiff or too soft. In general, if your zip tie is always showing close to maximum travel and adding some fork oil doesn't stop the front end from bottoming under braking, the front springs are too soft. Likewise, if the front end is constantly topping out even with the preload set at minimum, the spring is most likely too stiff. Front spring stiffness may also be a matter of personal preference; heavy brakers will prefer stiffer springs, whereas a rider that is more gentle on the binders will need softer springs to let the front end dive more when entering turns.

In most cases, you'll need a spring compressor to swap out the springs in a cartridge fork, and the process is dependent on the type of tool you use. Some allow you to change springs without removing the fork tubes from the bike, while others require some muscle, two people, and the forks out of the bike. Check your service manual for the tools required, or have a shop change the springs for you.

FORK OIL WEIGHT

In general, today's cartridge forks are intended to work with a specific viscosity of oil, and it's best to change the internal valving rather than use a heavier or lighter fluid. However, should your compression and rebound adjusters be consistently near the full-stiff or full-soft settings, one option to consider is a thicker or thinner fork oil viscosity. Few damping-rod forks offer any damping adjustments, and on bikes like the Suzuki SV650 or Kawasaki Ninja 650R, changing the fork fluid is the only way to adjust the damping. In days gone by, forks were equipped with drain screws at the bottom, and a fluid change would be a simple matter of carefully popping the caps off, draining the old, and filling each leg with the new. With cartridge forks (and even most current damping-rod forks, as manufacturers aren't bothering to fit drain screws), it's necessary to remove the individual fork legs to change the fluid. Follow your service manual for the correct method, and select oil that is thinner for less damping or thicker for more damping. It's possible to mix two oils for a personal blend; for instance, equal parts of 10- and 5-weight will be close enough to 7.5-weight. Just remember to write down the mix as well as the level you choose.

ABOVE: To properly change the fluid, most forks will have to be removed from the bike, and you may need a spring compressor to remove the cap and spring. Be sure to measure the fluid level before you drain the oil, and dispose of the old oil properly. (MARC COOK)

RIGHT: Follow the method in your service manual to change the oil, and set the level to what it was before the swap. (MARC COOK)

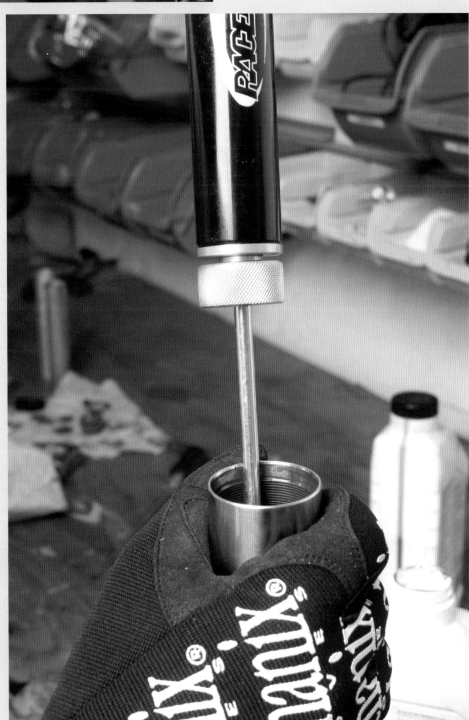

CHAPTER 11

Aftermarket Upgrades

Once you feel you've reached your stock suspension's potential, the aftermarket is standing by to help you upgrade or even replace your fork, shock, and other components with higher-performance items. The burning question is, of course, how do you know when you're at the limits of the stock parts? In some cases, the answer is simple: If you're, say, 110 pounds and using barely a quarter of the suspension's travel, you're a prime candidate for softer springs. In other cases, the answer is not so easy: I've seen bone stock bikes go pretty fast around a race track, and for some people the limit is pretty far out there. It really comes down to your experience, preferences, and ability to set up the stock suspension to your liking.

Be honest with yourself, and you'll most likely know when you're truly ready to upgrade to aftermarket components. In general, if you're not happy with your bike's handling and have exhausted all

setup avenues or are constantly running out of a particular adjustment range, it's time to modify. Be aware that making that decision and upgrading does not mean an end to the frustration; just bolting on a shock or revalving your fork will not automatically make you faster at your next track day. Those shiny new parts will require just as much setup attention as the stock bits they replaced. As well, keep in mind that even though you may not need to upgrade at present, it makes economic sense to consider all the options. For instance, if you're at the stage that softer or stiffer springs are required, it may save you money in the long run to have the fork and shock revalved at the same time the springs are installed, rather than taking everything apart twice.

As with any performance upgrade, it pays to conduct some research to get the most benefit from your hard-earned dollars. The biggest stumbling block for many riders when it comes to upgrading is that suspension modifications are often internal—or not easily noticed—and the changes don't affect the bike's appearance. It's tough to send your forks away for a several-hundred-dollar revalve when they come back looking, well . . . exactly the same, but for an additional sticker. Where's the fun in that?

Before making any modifications, ask other riders that have the same bike as you what upgrades they made and how that improved their bike's handling. A reputable suspension shop will make upgrade recommendations based on years of experience, as well as assist you in tuning your suspension after you make those upgrades. And check to see what product or service club racers in your area are using—that is often a good indication of what works and what is available locally.

The most common upgrade, and usually the best compromise in price/performance ratio, is an internal revalving of the stock shock and fork. This involves complete disassembly of the stock parts and replacing the shims that define your suspension's damping characteristics. In many cases, the shock piston (that the shims assemble to), or the complete valves in a cartridge fork, will be replaced with aftermarket components as well. The individual parts themselves—shims and valves or pistons—are relatively inexpensive, but with this modification, the bulk of the cost is knowledge and labor. The research and development that goes into shim stacks and valving is sometimes never-ending, and a good suspension shop will know from ongoing testing the best combinations that will work for you and your bike.

While it's possible to revalve a fork and shock yourself, it requires some special tools—including spring compressors, cartridge removers, and holders for forks—and you'll need even more to rebuild a shock. Unless you have all the tools necessary and are skilled and experienced at disassembling and assembling shocks and forks, I'd highly recommend you leave this upgrade to an expert. Not only will you be sure of having the job done right, but you'll also benefit from the shop's experience in making the final tuning adjustments.

A step beyond revalving the stock cartridge is a complete cartridge kit. These kits replace the entire stock cartridges with high-quality units that are oftentimes equal in performance to those found inside high-dollar aftermarket forks. A more-expensive alternative to revalving, cartridge kits are sometimes easier to install yourself, as they don't require disassembly of the stock units. Only a handful of companies currently offer the kits, but the technology is changing quickly enough that new and updated units are constantly being introduced.

If you absolutely must have an upgrade that is easily seen, nothing stands out quite as well as an aftermarket fork or shock, which completely replaces the stock components. A variety of manufacturers offer a number of models for different applications.

RIGHT: Owners of bikes with damping-rod forks can benefit from a popular Race Tech product called the *cartridge emulator*. This device (note the examples shown here are discolored with 15,000 miles of use) is installed on top of each fork's damping rod and makes the fork act in a similar manner to a cartridge fork. Unlike cartridge forks, damping-rod forks can be taken apart (and the emulator installed) with few special tools and moderate mechanical ability. (MARC COOK)

BELOW: Revalving the stock fork and shock internals can provide a significant performance increase for a moderate cash outlay, especially if you invest in the tools and do the work yourself. These GP Suspension valves replace the stock rebound and compression units inside a cartridge fork and come preassembled with shim stacks appropriate for a specific rider weight and experience. (ANDREW TREVITT)

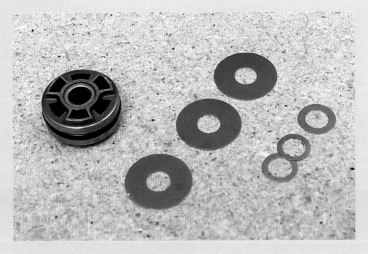

LEFT: Some companies offer kits with new pistons and a selection of shims, allowing you to assemble your own valving. A more cost-effective—but also more labor-intensive—option, the kit allows you to experiment with different shim stacks. (MARC COOK)

ABOVE: In production-based racing classes, the optimum setup is an aftermarket cartridge, which completely replaces the stock internals. (ADAM CAMPBELL)

LEFT: This aftermarket shock has better-quality internals than a stock unit and offers more adjustment possibilities. While most production shocks have preload, compression damping, and rebound damping adjustments, this Öhlins unit has high-speed compression damping and ride-height, in addition. (ADAM CAMPBELL)

BELOW: The adjustable triple clamps allow direct changes to trail without affecting rake. Inserts change the offset between the steering head and fork tubes, moving the wheel forward for less trail, rearward for more. (ADAM CAMPBELL)

One big benefit of an aftermarket shock is the addition of a length adjuster that allows you to change rear ride height without the need to change shims; that alone is a major plus when it comes time to make quick changes at the race track. Many shocks also have separate high- and low-speed compression damping adjusters, which will allow you to further fine-tune your bike's handling for a particular road or track.

Sometimes it's difficult to find a chassis balance that offers a good compromise in stability, steering, and squat characteristics, and this is when a set of adjustable triple clamps can come in handy. While the method differs between companies that manufacture the clamps, the end result is the same: The dimension between the steering stem and fork tubes—the offset—can be varied by a few millimeters in either direction from stock. This allows you to change trail independently of ride height and can be helpful in juggling steering and stability characteristics. Most race organizations do not allow aftermarket triple clamps in the production classes, but in Superbike they are permitted—and often a necessity when you're dealing with a 200hp literbike.

Stock rear shock linkages generally have a very progressive ratio, to stiffen the suspension further down in its travel and help prevent bottoming,

especially when a passenger is on board. Several companies manufacture links that are less progressive than the stock setup, providing more-consistent spring and damping characteristics over the course of the suspension's travel. Another adjustment that the aftermarket allows is changing the swingarm pivot height. On some bikes, such as the Suzuki GSX-R1000 and Triumph Daytona 675, inserts can be used to move the swingarm pivot in relation to the stock position. This lets the angle of the swingarm be adjusted to change squat characteristics independently of ride height. Again, aftermarket links and swingarm pivot inserts are not usually allowed in production-based classes.

While more adjustments give you more options to explore and improve your bike's handling, beware the downsides: There are exponentially more avenues to explore and increased potential for heading in a wrong setup direction. Troubleshooting a problem is infinitely more difficult when there are ten variables to consider instead of four or five. It's even more important to understand what each setting affects and to keep track of changes you make. I've seen many instances of riders going slower once they install an aftermarket shock or fork kit, simply because they were unable to properly dial in the new pieces.

CHAPTER 12

Troubleshooting Guide

Use this guide in conjunction with what you've learned in each chapter to help you identify and correct setup issues. Common symptoms are listed, along with likely causes and the recommended first steps to fixing the malady. Where more than one possible remedy is listed, the options are listed in order of preference. When dealing with handling problems, it helps to first identify in which area of the track or road the problem occurs: on a straight, under braking, entering a corner, midcorner, or exiting a corner.

ENTERING A CORNER

SYMPTOM	LIKELY CAUSE	POSSIBLE REMEDY
Steering is heavy and slow	Excessive trail	Reduce trail by raising the rear ride height, adding rear preload, raising the fork tubes in the triple clamps, reducing front preload, or increasing triple-clamp offset
Steering is quick and flighty or unstable	Insufficient trail	Add trail by lowering the rear ride height, reducing rear preload, lowering the fork tubes in the triple clamps, adding front preload, or decreasing triple-clamp offset
Steering is slow in side-to-side transitions	Center of gravity is too low	Raise center of gravity by lowering the fork tubes in the triple clamps and raising the rear ride height an equal amount
Chassis is unstable in side-to-side transitions	Insufficient rebound damping is allowing the chassis to unload excessively	Add front and rear rebound damping
Chassis is unstable in side-to-side transitions (continued)	Excessive compression damping is not allowing the chassis to settle	Reduce front and rear low-speed compression damping
Chassis resists leaning while trail braking	Insufficient rake	Increase rake by lowering rear ride height, reducing rear preload, lowering the fork tubes in the triple clamps, or adding front preload

MIDCORNER

SYMPTOM	LIKELY CAUSE	POSSIBLE REMEDY
High-frequency chatter	Tire is out of balance or out of round	Check tire condition
Footpegs or chassis parts drag	Center of gravity is too low	Raise center of gravity by lowering the fork tubes in the triple clamps and raising the rear ride height an equal amount, or increase front and rear spring rates
Ride is harsh and rough	Suspension is packing or bottoming	Reduce rebound damping, increase spring stiffness, or increase preload
Ride is bouncy and loose	Insufficient rebound damping	Add front and rear rebound damping
Limited traction over bumps	Suspension is too stiff	Reduce rebound damping, reduce low- or high-speed compression damping, or reduce preload

EXITING A CORNER

SYMPTOM	LIKELY CAUSE	POSSIBLE REMEDY
Bike runs wide or is unstable over bumps	Excessive squat is causing the front tire to lose traction	Reduce squat by adding rear low-speed compression damping, adding rear preload, adding rear ride height, raising the fork tubes in the triple clamps, adding front rebound damping, or raising the swingarm pivot
Sudden loss of rear traction on acceleration	Insufficient squat	Increase squat by reducing rear low-speed compression damping, reducing rear preload, reducing rear ride height, lowering the fork tubes in the triple clamps, reducing front rebound damping, or lowering the swingarm pivot
Excessive wheelies	Center of gravity is too high	Raise the fork tubes in the triple clamps and lower the rear ride height an equal amount
Excessive chassis pitching	Excessive weight transfer	Add rear low-speed compression damping, add rear high-speed compression damping, reduce front rebound damping, or lower the center of gravity

STRAIGHT

SYMPTOM	LIKELY CAUSE	POSSIBLE REMEDY
Wallows over rolling bumps	Insufficient compression damping	Add low-speed compression damping
Bottoms out in depressions	Insufficient high-speed compression damping	Add high-speed compression damping
Harsh over sharp-edged bumps	Excessive compression damping	Decrease high-speed compression damping or low-speed compression damping
Wobble (high-frequency headshake) on smooth pavement	Insufficient trail	Add trail by lowering rear ride height, reducing rear preload, lowering the fork tubes in the triple clamps, adding front preload, or decreasing triple-clamp offset
Wobble (high-frequency headshake) on rough pavement	Excessive squat is allowing the front end to unload	Reduce squat by adding rear low-speed compression damping, adding rear preload, raising rear ride height, raising the fork tubes in the triple clamps, or raising the swingarm pivot
Weave (low-frequency headshake)	Insufficient rear damping is allowing the rear end to oscillate	Add rear rebound or low-speed compression damping
Suspension gets progressively harsher over a series of bumps	Excessive rebound damping is allowing the suspension to pack down	Reduce rebound damping
Chassis feels loose and loses traction or is unstable over rough pavement	Insufficient rebound damping	Add rebound damping

BRAKING

SYMPTOM	LIKELY CAUSE	POSSIBLE REMEDY
Rear wheel comes off the ground or slides sideways	Excessive rear rebound damping is allowing the wheel to leave the ground	Reduce rear rebound damping
Excessive chassis pitch	Insufficient damping to control brake dive	Add front low-speed compression damping or add rear rebound damping
Excessive chassis pitch (continued)	Center of gravity is too high	Lower the center of gravity by raising the fork tubes in the triple clamps and lowering the rear ride height an equal amount
Front end feels harsh at maximum braking	Fork is bottoming	Add front low-speed compression damping, add fork oil, add front preload, or increase front spring rate
Lack of feel from front end	Not enough weight is transferring to the front tire	Remove fork oil, reduce front low-speed compression damping, or reduce front preload
Lack of feel from front end (continued)	Insufficient trail	Increase trail by lowering the rear ride height, reducing rear preload, lowering the fork tubes in the triple clamps, adding front preload, or decreasing triple-clamp offset
Front end bounces when the brakes are released, giving a momentary loss of traction	Insufficient front rebound damping	Add front rebound damping

Glossary

BOTTOMING: Occurs when the fork or shock is fully compressed.

COMPRESSION DAMPING: A force that prevents the fork or shock from compressing, relative to the velocity of the compression.

DAMPING: A force that restricts movement, proportional to the velocity of the movement.

DIVE: Compression of the front fork due to weight transfer, usually under braking.

FORK OIL LEVEL: A measure of how much air is left in a fork tube, expressed as a dimension from the top of the fork tube to the oil with the fork and cartridge compressed and the spring removed.

FORK OIL WEIGHT: The viscosity of oil used in the fork.

FREE SAG: A measure of how much a bike's suspension is compressed from fully extended under its own weight.

GEOMETRY: A motorcycle's overall geometry is defined by the combination of rake, trail, and ride-height measurements, all of which interact with each other.

HIGH-SPEED DAMPING: Affects the movement of the fork or shock at high shaft speeds. Examples are freeway expansion joints, sharp-edged bumps, and rough pavement.

LINKAGE: A system of levers used to vary the ratio of wheel movement to shock compression over the span of the wheel's travel.

LOW-SPEED DAMPING: Affects the movement of the fork or shock at low shaft speeds. Examples are rolling bumps, dive under braking, and squat under acceleration.

OFFSET: A dimension from the steering axis to a plane defined by the front fork tubes. Most triple clamps are machined such that the fork tubes are parallel to the steering head, in which case offset is easily measured. In rare cases that the two are not parallel, offset must be expressed in terms of a distance and an angle.

PACKING: Occurs when excessive rebound damping prevents a fork or shock from extending to its original length (after it is compressed by a bump) before the next bump is encountered. The fork or shock com-presses progressively deeper into its stroke over a succession of bumps, potentially bottoming.

PRELOAD: The distance a spring is compressed from its free length when it is installed in a fork or shock. For example, a 315mm fork spring, installed in a fork tube that has 300mm of space for the spring, has 15mm of preload.

RAKE: The angle of the steering axis from vertical.

REBOUND DAMPING: A force that prevents the fork or shock from extending, relative to the velocity of the extension.

RIDE HEIGHT: A measure of the height of the motorcycle directly above the front or rear axle. Front ride height can be adjusted by sliding the fork tubes in the triple clamps, while rear ride height can be changed by extending or shortening the shock or its linkage.

SAG (SOMETIMES CALLED RIDER SAG): A measure of how much a bike's suspension is compressed from fully extended when the rider is aboard.

SPRING RATE: A measure of a spring's stiffness, in dimensions of kg/mm, N/mm, or lb./in.

SPRUNG WEIGHT: The portion of the motorcycle that is suspended.

SQUAT: Compression of the rear suspension due to weight transfer or chain pull, usually under acceleration.

STEERING DAMPER: Generally a hydraulic device used to slow the front end's rotation around the steering axis.

TOPPING: Occurs when the fork or shock is fully extended.

TRAIL: The horizontal distance from the steering axis to the center of the front tire's contact patch.

UNSPRUNG WEIGHT: The portion of the motorcycle that is not suspended, including the wheels, brakes, and parts of the swingarm, fork, and shock.

WEAVE: Instability at the rear of the motorcycle, generally characterized by an oscillation of 2–3 cycles per second.

WHEELBASE: A horizontal dimension between the front and rear axles.

WOBBLE: Instability at the front of the motorcycle, generally characterized by an oscillation of 10 cycles per second.

Index

Page numbers in *italics* refer to
photographs and captions

A

Acceleration
  and anti-squat, 79, 81
  and rear traction, 79
  and squat, 79
  and weight transfer, 43, 79
Anti-squat, 79–83
  and acceleration, 79, 81
  decreasing, *4*, 83
  forces involved, 79–80, *81*
  increasing, 83
  in shaft drive motorcycles, *4*
  and swingarm angle, 83, 95
  and swingarm pivot, *82*, 83, *83*

B

Bearings
  inspection of, *18, 19,* 21
BMW motorcycles, *4–5,* 80
Bottoming
  definition, 46, 126
  troubleshooting, 124
Braking
  fork bottoming remedies, 108
  front-end dive, 28, 43, 57, 76
  front rebound damping test,
    68, 71
  rear rebound damping test, 71
  and spring stiffness, 114
  troubleshooting, 123, 125
Bridgestone BT-015 tires, 86, *88*
Buell motorcycles
  interaction between
    compression and rebound
    circuits, 66
  tires, 89

C

C-wrench
  for preload adjustment, 21–22,
    22, 47, *49*
Cartridge forks
  aftermarket kits, 118
  aftermarket valves, *119*
  changing fork oil, 114
  changing springs, *110,* 114
  disassembly tools, *111*
  revalving, 118
Chain
  and anti-squat, 79, 80–91, *81,* 83
  impact of sprocket size, *78, 79*
  pull forces, 80–81
  in rear-end geometry, *40, 41,* 80
  tension, 21, *40, 41*
Chassis
  inspection, 18, 21
Chatter
  troubleshooting, 123
Clevis shims, 38, *38,* 105–6, *107*
Compression damping
  adjuster location, *54, 55, 69,* 72
  adjustment, 62, *62, 63,* 71–73,
    75–76
  baseline settings, 75
  basics, 59–60
  definition, 28, *28,* 126
  forces, *56*
  and fork oil weight, 114
  front and rear balance, 75, *75*
  high-speed, *54, 55,* 60, 62, *69,*
    72, 75, 76, 77
  impact on geometry, 75–76
  interaction with rebound
    damping, 65–66

low-speed, *54, 55, 64, 65, 69,*
    72, 73, 75, 76, 76, 77
  settings, 18, 72–73, 75
  testing, 75, *75*
  and wheel weight, 71–72
Cornering
  and sag settings, 48
  spring compression, 43
  testing front rebound damping,
    68, 71

  troubleshooting, 122–23

D

Damping, 55–76
  adjusters, 27, *66,* 97, 99, 114
  adjustment tools, *22*
  and anti-squat, 83
  basics, 55–57, 59
  compression (*see* Compression
    damping)
  definition, 26, 126
  forces, *56*
  and fork oil, *18,* 56–57, 60, 114
  friction, 55
  and geometry, 100
  high-speed components, 57, 59
  hydraulic, 55
  low-speed components, 57, 59
  rebound (*see* Rebound damping)
  testing, *70, 71, 73, 75*
Damping-rod forks
  cartridge emulator, *119*
  fork oil and damping, 57
  swapping springs, *110*
Dive
  causes, 28
  definition, 126
Driving force, 79–80, *80*
Ducati motorcycles
  adjustable rake, 31
  adjustable steering-head insert,
    34, 35
  compression adjusters, *66, 67*
  ride-height adjustment, *36,*
    37, *37*
  steering and stability, 33
  tools, *66, 67*
Dunlop D220 tires, 85

E

Eccentric axle clamps
  and rear ride height, *40, 41*

F

Flat-blade screwdriver
  for adjusting rebound, 21, 57, 65
Fluid dynamics, 56
Fork caps
  with adjusters, *11*
  changing fluid, *115*
  compression damping adjusters,
    72
  front preload adjuster, 51
  removal, *105, 115*
Fork oil
  changing, 18, *18, 105, 109,*
    114, *115*
  definitions, 126
  and fork travel, *106*
  level, 106, 108, 126
  relationship of volume to
    height, *109*
  removing, *6,* 108, *109*
  weight, 114, 126
Fork tubes
  cautions, 40
  changing fluid, *105, 109, 115*
  compression, 52–53
  compression and effective
    spring rate, 106, *106,* 108
  compression damping adjusters,

66, 67, 72
height adjustment instructions,
    39
height and geometry, *33, 34,* 35,
    37, 105
height and preload, *52, 53,* 99
height and tire size, 90, *91*
and spring compression, *106*
spring size and preload, 43–44
and steering, 99
travel, 76, *106,* 108
travel measurement, *96, 97,*
    106, 114
Forks
  aftermarket, *116, 117,* 118
  aftermarket springs, *110*
  bottoming prevention, 108
  cartridge, *111*
  compression damping forces, *56*
  damping adjusters, *57,* 60, *64, 65*
  diving, 76
  friction in, 47
  maintenance, 18
  revalving, 118, *119*
  topping out over bumps, 95
Free sag
  definition, 48, 126
  and spring rate, 111–12
  and steering, 99
Friction
  damping, 55
  in the suspension, 47
Front damping
  checking, 68, *70,* 71, *71*
  compression, 72, 75
  rebound, 62, 68, 71
Front dive
  causes, 28
  definition, 126
Front preload
  adjustment, 43, 48, 51, *51*
  adjustment tools, 22
  and geometry, 99–100
  settings, *99*
  see also Preload
Front ride height
  raising, 105
  see also Ride height
Front sag
  guidelines, 48
  measurement, *46,* 51, 97
  and preload, 99–100
  see also Sag
Front springs
  stiffness, 114
  see also Springs
Front sprockets
  and anti-squat, 83
  cautions, *79*
  size, 78, *79,* 83
  see also Sprockets
Front traction
  for steering, 79

G

Gearing changes
  impact on rear ride height,
    40, 41
Geometry
  adjusting, 99
  and anti-squat, 83
  definition, 126
  impact of compression
    damping, 75–76
  impact of suspension
    adjustment, 34
  influence on steering, 33–34
  overview, 31
  and preload, 51–53, 99–100
  rake and trail adjustment, *32,*
    33, 33

testing impact of changes, 35
Glossary, 126

H

High-speed damping
  compression, *54, 55,* 60, 62, *69,*
    72, 75, 76, 77
  definition, 28, 126
  rebound, 60
Honda motorcycles
  cam timing experiments, 14
  data-acquisition sensors for
    setting sag, *45*
  Honda CB175, 10, 55
  Honda CBR900RR, 14
  Honda CBR1000RR, *45,* 88
  Honda ST1300, *50*
  hydraulic preload adjuster, *50*
  ramped preload adjusters, *47*
  steering damper, 55
  tires, *88*
  Unit Pro-Link setup, 38
Hydraulic damping, 55

K

Kawasaki motorcycles
  aftermarket shims, 106, *107*
  anti-squat forces, *81*
  clevis shims, *38, 107*
  compression adjuster location,
    62
  interaction between
    compression and rebound
    circuits, 66
  Kawasaki Ninja 650R, 114
  Kawasaki Z1000, 62
  Kawasaki ZX-6R, 38, 66, *81*
  Kawasaki ZX-10R, 38
  preload adjustment, 47
  rebound adjuster location, 62
  ride-height adjustment, 38, *38*
Kayaba forks
  interaction between
    compression and rebound
    circuits, 66

L

Linkage
  bearings, *18*
  definition, 126
  measuring ratio, 37–38
Literbikes
  importance of suspension
    tuning, 13
Low-speed damping
  compression, *54, 55, 64, 65, 69,*
    72, 73, 75, 76, 76, 77
  definition, 28, 126
  and rear-end squat, 76

M

McMaster-Carr shims, 106
Michelin Pilot Power 2CT tires, 86
Moto Guzzi motorcycles
  compression adjuster location,
    62
  rebound adjuster location, 62
MV Agusta motorcycles
  damping adjusters, 62, 65
  fork cap and adjusters, *11*
  shocks, 62

N

Note taking
  baseline settings, 96
  compression damping
    adjustments, 73, 75
  format, 22, 96–97, *97*
  importance, 22
  rebound damping adjustments,
    68
  ride-height adjustments, 40
  samples, 101–3

O

OEM tires, 85, *86,* 89
Offset
  definition, 126
Öhlins
  aftermarket fork, *116, 117*
  aftermarket shocks, 48, *50, 66,*
    67, 120
Oil
  damping, 56–57, 60
Orifice damping, *56,* 56–57, 59, 60

P

Packing
  definition, 126
Pirelli Diablo tires, 86, 89
Pit Bull jack stands, *112, 113*
Pre-ride check, 99
Preload
  adjustment tools, 22, *22,* 49
  adjustments, 43, 47–48, *48, 49,*
    51, *51, 52, 53,* 95
  definition, 43, 126
  experiments, 53
  and fork tubes, *53,* 99
  and geometry, 51–53, 95, 99–100
  hydraulic adjusters, *50*
  measurement, 50
  ramped adjusters, 47
  and ride height, 95, 97, 99
  and road surface, 53
  and sag, 47, 51, 99, 112
  settings, *99*
  and springs, 26, 43–44, *44,* 52
  and squat, 100
  and stability, 95
  stepped-collar adjusters, 47
  and suspension, 44, 46

R

Race Tech
  cartridge emulator, *119*
  cartridge fork, *111*
  preload tool, *49*
  sag measurement, 46
Racing bikes
  anti-squat, 81
  front sag settings, 48
  production-based class rules,
    121
  rear sag settings, 47
  setting differences from street
    bikes, 48, 51
  spring stiffness, 112
  tire choice, 85, *86, 87*
  tire pressure, *88,* 92, 93
Rake
  adjustment, 31, *33*
  and compression damping, 76
  definition, 28, 31, 126
  diagram, *29*
  and ride height, 35, 37, 99
Rear damping
  and braking, 71
  checking, *73*
  rebound, 71
  see also Damping
Rear geometry, 31, *80*
Rear preload
  adjusting, *49*
  and geometry, 99–100
  ramped adjusters, 47
  and sag, 99, 112
  and springs, 43
  tools, 22, *22*
  see also Preload
Rear ride height
  adjustment, 37, 105–6
  measuring changes, 37–38
  and tire size, 90
  see also Ride height

Rear sag
  measurement, 97
  and preload, 99–100
  reference point, *42, 43*
  see also Sag
Rear shocks
  adjuster location, *62, 69, 72*
  aftermarket linkages, 121
  compression damping settings, 75
  free sag, 99
  inspection, 21
  linkage and bearings, 21
  removal, *112, 113*
  see also Shocks
Rear springs
  changing, 112
  see also Springs
Rear sprockets
  size and anti-squat, 83
  see also Sprockets
Rear squat, 28, 76
  see also Squat
Rear suspension
  friction in, 47
Rear traction
  for acceleration, 79
  see also Traction
Rear wheel travel
  measuring, *94, 95, 96*, 99
Rebound damping
  adjustment, *61, 62, 62, 63*, 65–66, 68, 71
  baseline setting, 66, 68
  basics, 59–60
  definition, 28, *28*, 126
  and fork oil weight, 114
  and handling, 68
  high-speed, 60
  interaction with compression damping, 65–66
  measurement, 97
  note taking, 68
  screw-type adjusters, *58, 59*
  testing, 68, 71
Ride
  troubleshooting, 122, 124
Ride height
  adjustment, 31, *36, 37*, 37–38, *40, 41*, 99, *107*
  adjustment experiments, 38
  and chain tension, 40, *41*
  definition, 126
  front, 105
  and gear changes, 40
  and geometry, *34, 35*, 37, 38, 40
  and linkage ratio, 37
  and preload, 53, 95, 97, 99
  rear, *40, 41*
  shock clevis shim, 105–6, *107*
  and squat, 100
  and tire size, 90, *91*
Rider sag. *see* Sag
Road Atlanta, *8, 9*
Roadracing
  importance of suspension tuning, 9
  monoshock rear end, 10
Road surface
  preload adjustment, 53

S

Safety
  and suspension tuning, *13*
Sag
  adjusting, 53
  and anti-squat, *81*
  definition, 46, 126
  front, *46*, 48, 51, 97, 99–100
  measurement, *45, 46*, 46–47, 51, 97
  and preload, 47–48, 99–100, 112

rear sag, *42, 43*, 97, 99–100
  setting, *42, 43*, 45, 46, 47–48
  and spring rate, 111–12
Screwdrivers
  for adjusting rebound, 21, *57*, 65
Seals
  maintenance, 18
Shaft drive motorcycles
  anti-squat, *4*, 80
Shim-stack damping, *56*, 60, 118, *119*
Shims
  adding under shock clevis, *107*
  aftermarket, 38, 106, *119*
  for ride-height adjustment, 38, *38*, 105–6
Shock linkage
  adjustable-length rod, *36, 37*
  aftermarket, *121*
Shocks
  adjustment limits, 40
  aftermarket, 37, 118, *120*, 121
  and body weight, 48
  clevis shims, 38, *38*, 105–6, *107*
  compression damping, *56*, 60, *69, 120*
  fluid, 18
  friction, 47
  height adjustment, 37
  inspection of bearings, 21
  maintenance, 18
  preload adjustment, 47–48
  with ramp-type adjuster, 112
  rebound damping, *58, 59*, 60, *61*
  remote hydraulic units, 48
  replacing, 112, *112*, 114
  revalving, 118, *119*
  ride-height adjustment, 37, *120*
  shaft, *94, 95*, 97
  spring rate, 25
  with threaded rings for preload, 112
  with two springs, 25
Showa forks, 66
Socket wrenches
  for adjusting front preload, 22
Sport Rider
  changing test bike's settings, 17
  road tests, 96
  variations in riders, 17
Sport-touring motorcycles
  hydraulic preload adjusters, *50*
  shocks with remote hydraulic units, 48
Sportbikes
  anti-squat, 81, *81*
  damping, *57*, 60
  damping-rod forks, 57
  rake, *30, 31*, 34, 35, 37
  springs, 46, *110*
  stock adjustments, 95
  suspension tuning kit, 9
  tires, 85–86, 88, 89
  trail, *30, 31, 31, 34*
Spring compressor, 112, *112*, 114, *115*
Spring rate
  definition, 126
Springs
  aftermarket, *110*, 117
  changing, *110, 112*, 114, *115*
  coil bind, 25
  compression, *25, 26, 26, 28*, 43
  controlling distance of wheel movement, 28
  force, *106*, 108
  and fork compression, 106, *106*, 108
  free length, *44*
  front, 114
  function, 25–26

and preload, *24, 25*, 43–44, *44*, 52
  progressive, 25
  for racing, 112
  rear spring rate, 48
  and rider weight, 48, 108, 111, 117
  and sag, 111–12
  stiffness, *25*, 46, 112, 114
  stock, *110*
  vibration frequency, 26
Sprockets
  and anti-squat, 79, 80, 81, 83
  cautions, *79*
  front, *78, 79*, 83
  size, *78, 79*, 83
Sprung weight
  definition, 126
Squat, 79–83
  under acceleration, 79
  definition, 126
  impact of ride height and preload, 100
  rear-end, 76
Stability
  compromise with steering, 99
  impact of ride-height adjustment, 40
  troubleshooting, 122, 124
Steering
  adjustable, *34, 35*
  adjusting, 99
  and anti-squat, 81, 83
  and damping, 34
  and free sag, 99
  front traction, 79
  and geometry, 33–34
  for novice riders, 33
  and preload, 34
  and ride height, 40
  slow steering causes, 18
  and stability, 33–34, 99
  and tires, 89
  troubleshooting, 122
Steering head
  angle, *28, 29*
  bearing inspection, 18, 21
  bearings, 18, *18*
Street bikes
  changing fork oil, *18*
  damping, *18*
  front sag settings, 48
  geometry and stability, 30, 31, *31*
  importance of suspension tuning, *13*
  rear sag settings, 47
  setting differences from racing bikes, 48, 51
  tire pressure, 92–93
Superbike
  and anti-squat, 81
  rules, 121
Suspension tuning
  baseline settings, 95–96
  compromises, 17–18
  by factory team, *14, 15*
  goals, 97
  impact on lap times, 9, 13
  impact on ride, 17
  impact on safety, *13*
  importance of testing and recording impact of changes, 14, 17, *22, 23*
  tools, 9, *22*
  trackside services, 95–96
Suzuki motorcycles
  aftermarket shims, 38, *38*
  compression damping, *54, 55*, 71–72
  interaction between compression and rebound circuits, 66
  preload adjustment, 47

ride-height adjustment, 38, *38*
  Suzuki GSX-R models, 38
  Suzuki GSX-R1000, *54, 55*, 66, 71–72, *82, 83*, 121
  Suzuki SV650, 114
  swingarm pivot, *82, 83*
Suzuki SV Cup finals, Road Atlanta (2003), *8, 9*
Swingarm
  angle, 31, 79, 81, 83, 95, 100
  and anti-squat, 79, 81, *81, 82*, 83, *83, 95*
  bearings, *18*, 21
  pivot, *82, 83*
  pivot height, 79, 81, 83, 121
  shock removal, *112*
  and squat, 100
  tire-pressure recommendations, *88*

T

Tension damping. *see* Rebound damping
Thede, Paul, 46, 96
Tires, 85–93
  and chassis setup, 86
  construction, 86
  DOT-race, *84, 85, 85*, 86, *86*, 89
  gauges, *86*
  and geometry, 13, 17
  and handling, 85
  high-performance sport, *84, 85, 85, 86*
  hybrid street/track, 85, 86
  labeling, 89
  measuring, 90
  measuring clearance, *96*
  note taking, *17*
  performance chart, *89*
  pressure, 18, *20*, 21, *21*
  pressure recommendations, *88*, 92–93
  racing, *86, 87*, 92
  and ride feel, 89
  and ride height, 90, *91*
  size, 90, *91*
  slick, *84, 85, 85*, 86, 89
  sport, *84, 85*, 85–86, 89, 92
  sport-touring, *84, 85, 85*, 89
  sportbikes, 85
  and stability, 89, 92
  and steering, 18
  and suspension, *17*, 21
  traction, 89, 92
  tread, *84, 85*, 86
  types, *84, 85*, 89
  warmers, 92
Titanium nitride, *117*
Tools
  Allen key, 66, *67*
  C-wrench, 21–22, *22*, 47, *49*
  screwdrivers, 21, *57*, 65
Topper
  definition, 126
Track surface
  adjusting preload, 53
Track type
  and suspension, 10
Traction
  and anti-squat, 81
  front, 79
  rear, 79
  and steering, 79
  troubleshooting, 123
Trail
  adjustment, 31, *33*, 121
  and compression damping, 76
  definition, 28, 31, 126
  diagram, *29*
  and preload, 95
  and ride height, *34, 35*, 37, 38, 40

Trevitt, Andrew
  Suzuki SV Cup (2003), *8, 9*
Triple clamps, *33*
  adjustable, *120*, 121
  aftermarket, *120*, 121
  cautions, 40
  and fork tubes, *34*, 37, 52, *53*
  regulations, 121
Triumph motorcycles
  compression adjuster location, 6
  rebound adjuster location, 62
  Triumph Daytona 675, 121
  Triumph Speed Triple, 62
Troubleshooting, 122–25

U

Unsprung weight
  definition, 126

V

Valves
  aftermarket, *119*
  damping, 60
  kits, *119*
Velocity
  relationship to damping, 57, 59

W

Weave
  definition, 126
Wheel bearings, *18*, 21
Wheel weight
  and compression damping, 71–7
Wheelbase
  definition, 126
Wobble
  definition, 126

Y

Yamaha motorcycles
  aftermarket shims, 38, *38*
  compression damping, 62, *62, 63, 69, 76, 77*
  monoshock rear end, 10
  ramped adjusters for rear preload, 47
  rear shocks, 69
  rebound damping, 62, *62, 63*
  ride-height adjustment, 38, *38*
  steering, 33
  three-position front preload cap, 10
  tire pressure, 93
  Yamaha FZ1, 62, *62, 63*
  Yamaha R6, 33, *76, 77*
  Yamaha R series, 38
  Yamaha TZ250, 10
  Yamaha TZ250S, 21
  Yamaha YZF-R6, *69*, 93

Z

Zemke, Jake, *45*
Zip ties
  to measure fork travel, 97, *106*, 114
  to measure rear wheel travel, *95, 96*
  to measure suspension travel, 51, *52*, 76